SYMMETRICAL STICKINGS

FOR SNARE DRUM, DRUM SET & PERCUSSION

PETE LOCKETT

HUDSON MUSIC®

2018 FOREWORD - DOM FAMULARO

I have the fun role of traveling around the world performing, teaching and sharing the joy of drumming. On these trips I have observed a common personality trait I see in drummers globally. That is the desire to always challenge themselves to learn new ideas in stick movement!

It amazes me that in every corner of the world, that learning search is a constant. With different sticking patterns, we open doors of musical ideas. These ideas help us formulate our personal distinct sound, our unique set up and our individual style!

I have traveled the globe with Pete Lockett and have witnessed first hand him play different patterns and sounds at every performance. His percussion voice is distinctive, his set up creative, and his style is one in a million! His stickings, whether played with his hands or with drum sticks provides a vast knowledge of diverse options. It amazes me every time I hear him. Pete constantly challenges himself!

Well, he placed these ideas in this book, SYMMETRICAL STICKINGS, having been requested by many drummer's to share these creative sparks. This is now an open door, available for you to travel through into new dimensions of sticking possibilities!

Personally, I also enjoy playing these with my feet. The double bass ideas are endless and develop many different ways of thinking using feet and hand combinations!

Once you have journeyed with Stick Control by George L. Stone, you can continue with SYMMETRICAL STICKINGS by Pete Lockett! 21st century playing requires 21st century ideas! I feel Pete has built on what came before us in a way to push our potential.

He explores in a 'balance of movement' with equal playing for both hands and feet! I also like the odd time exposure to stickings, creating a new set of performance options!

Hop aboard and take the Lockett Rocket ride to a different sticking universe! We look forward to meeting you on your journey as we pass on the roads of musical expression.

Thanks so much.

Dom Famularo - Drumming's Global Ambassador

New York 2018

ORIGINAL FOREWORD - BILL BRUFORD

Paradiddles have a lousy name. They bear the only technical name in percussion known to the wilfully unknowledgeable, who think it is hilarious that we drummers should examine such things at close quarters.

Young drummers shudder at the memory of trying to master the harmless little guy in their early lessons. Most players get the single, double, triple and perhaps the paradiddlediddle down in their primary inversions and move hurriedly on, thus missing the endless stream of possible, and in this book, symmetrical, variations that are so user friendly and musical when applied around the drumset.

Just when you think theres not much more you can do with a paradiddle, Lockett comes along with this deceptively simple looking volume that will keep you busy for years. He examines the rudiment and its close cousins in an organised and methodological manner, generating exciting rhythms in not only 4/4 and 6/8, but also the less common 5/4 and 7/4 metres. Since the second half of each exersise is symmetrical "mirror image" of the first half, both hands get an equal work out.

Paradiddles are at the basis of many a fascinating rhythm. Wether you know it or not, chances are you are unsing them somewhere. Some drummers tend primarily to use the single stroke style (Most phrases played with alternate sticking), others the double stroke (two beats with each stick). Mastery of the paradiddle, being the simplest possible combination of the two, will blur that distinction and offer an invaluable third way to execute the phrase.

Follow this book as far as it will lead you, and your efforts will be amply rewarded.

Bill Bruford. British drumming icon

Surrey UK. 2009

CONTENTS PAGE

SYMMETRICAL STICKINGS

WHAT IS THIS BOOK ABOUT?

This book is part one of a three part series looking at sticking patterns applied to the snare drum, drum set and congas.

The content of the series focuses on sticking patterns derived from the symmetrical concept of the paradiddle, where the second half of the sticking is the exact opposite of the first half.

WHAT CAN I GAIN FROM LEARNING THESE STICKING PATTERNS?

A question I've heard so many times from students is "What's the point in getting paradiddle type rudiments together? I really can't see a way of using them in everyday playing." It's amazing how quickly they come around when you begin to show them some of the possible applications across any style of music.

Whether you're developing a funk groove, playing a four bar Jazz break or hitting a 'Keith Moon' rock solo, these styles of rudiments are indispensable. Drummers as varied as Steve Gadd, Elvin Jones and Keith Moon have all made great use of them.

THE PARADIDDLE, WHAT IS IT?

The Paradiddle is basically a sticking pattern, with the second half the exact opposite of the first half.

Note: All left hand players will need to reverse all stickings:

Right Handed Players

R L R R L R L L

Left Handed Players

L R L L R L R R

WHAT CAN IT ADD TO MY PLAYING?

Using stickings such as these can lead in many different directions; creating interesting accent patterns/articulating patterns on a number of drums that would be impossible with singles strokes/giving a good workout to both hands equally/creating complex sounding patterns between Hi Hat and Snare or lyrical patterns using Snare and Toms. The applications are endless.

THE BASIC PARADIDDLE

Here we have some of the basic paradiddles with accents.

SINGLE PARADIDDLE

R L R R L R L L

DOUBLE PARADIDDLE

R L R L R R L R L R L L

TRIPLE PARADIDDLE

R L R L R L R R L R L R L R L L

THE BASIC PARADIDDLE STARTING IN DIFFERENT PLACES

Here we have the basic paradiddles with accents, starting from a different note in the paradiddle each time.

1)

R L R R L R L L

2)

R L L R L R R L

3)

R R L R L L R L

4)

R L R L L R L R

LONGER THEME AND INVERSION STICKING PATTERNS

Using this concept we can now begin to construct some longer sticking patterns. Theoretically they can be any length, as long as they split in half, with the second half the exact opposite of the first half.

The first half of the following example is one bar of 16th's long and is divided into two groups of six and one group of four. (The bar could be divided into any subdivision to make up the total time space, i.e. $5 + 5 + 6 = 16$, is an alternative).

Here are the rudiments I've used for the groups;

Example 1 First Half

1st group of 6; 1st half of double paradiddle,
2nd group of 6; 2nd half of double paradiddle,
Group of 4; 1st half of paradiddle

Example 1 Second Half

1st group of 6; 2nd half of double paradiddle,
2nd group of 6; 1st half of double paradiddle,
Group of 4; 2nd half of paradiddle

Here is what it looks like:

1st Half

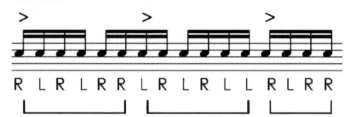

2nd Half

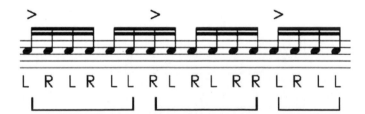

Note: The Second Half is the complete opposite of First Half.

This is the method that is the cornerstone of the concept of this set of books. Notice how I've indicated each group of the subdivisions by the markings underneath the score. This will help understand how the examples in the book are constructed.

OTHER STICKING PATTERNS USED IN THIS BOOK

Also, other hybrid sticking patterns of odd lengths, derived from paradiddles that have been used in this book.

Here are some examples;

5 Strokes Long

R L R L L

7 Strokes Long

R L L R R L R

9 Strokes Long

R L R L L R L R L

There are also sticking patterns using triple strokes. These are a little more tricky to articulate smoothly but are invaluable in developing stick control.

R L L L R R R L

R L L L R L L L R R R L R R R L

16ᵗʰ PATTERNS IN 4/4

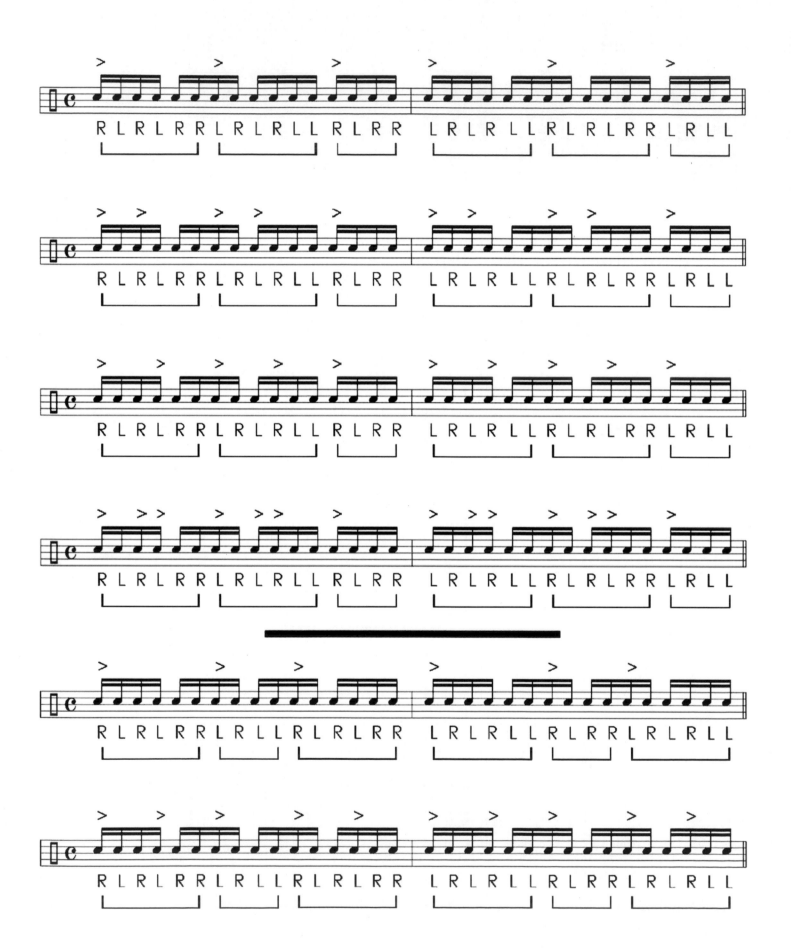

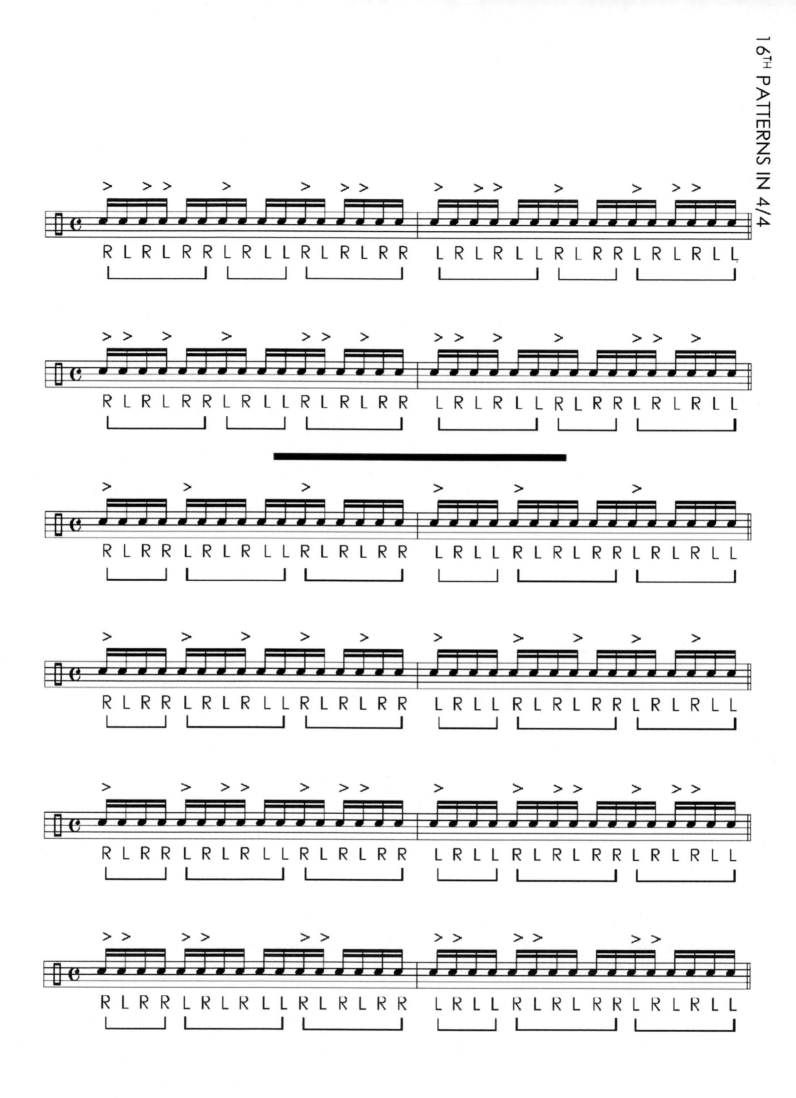

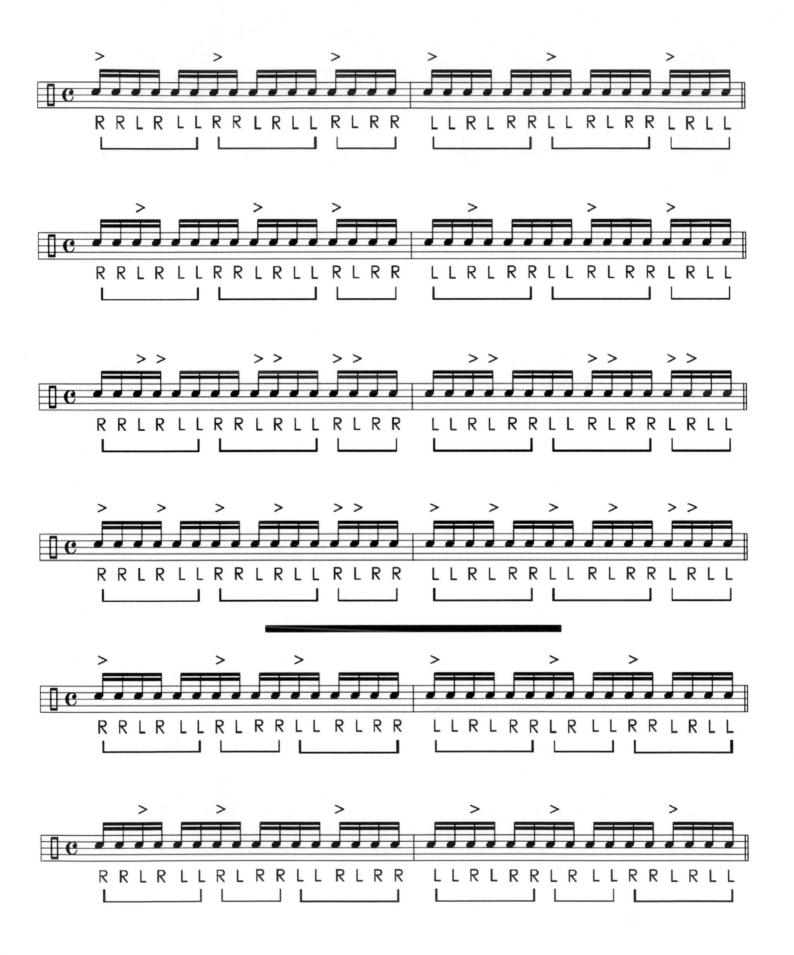

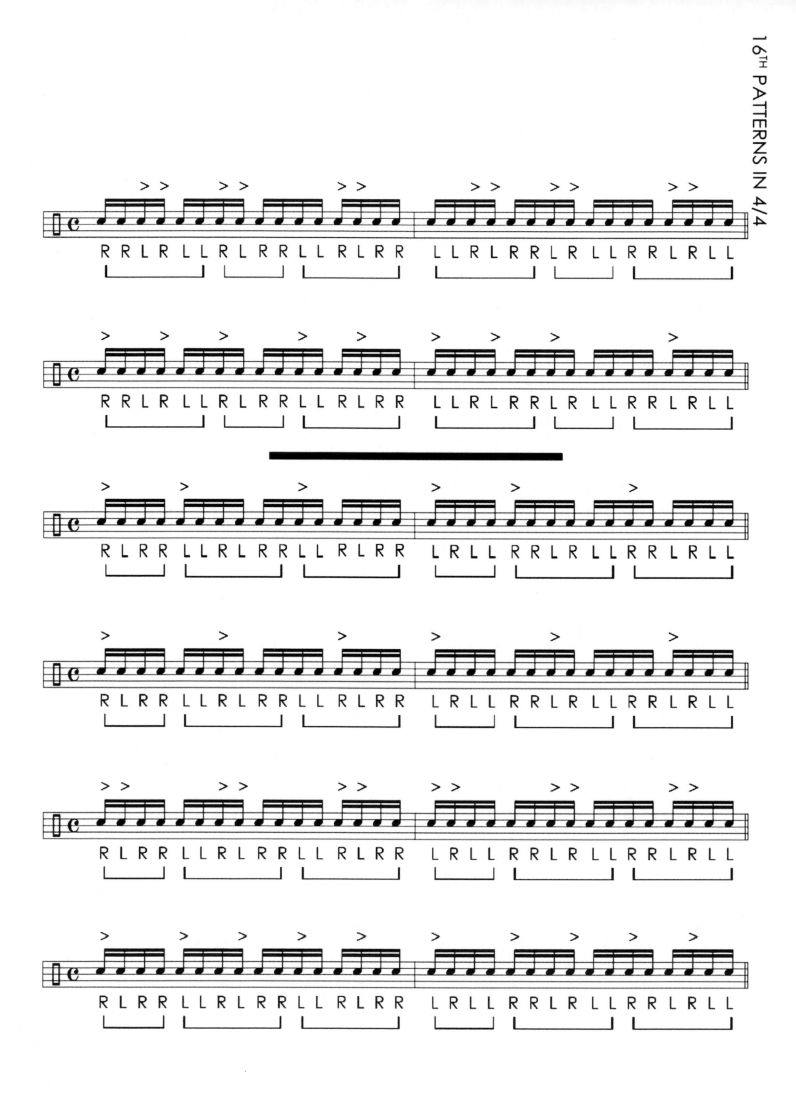

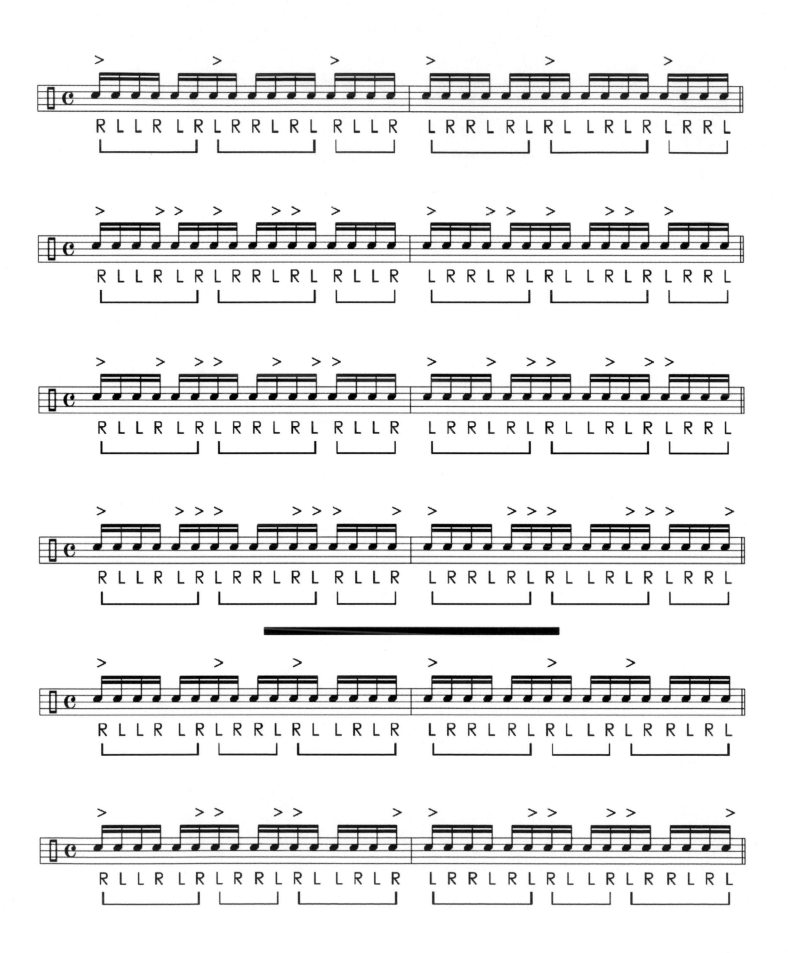

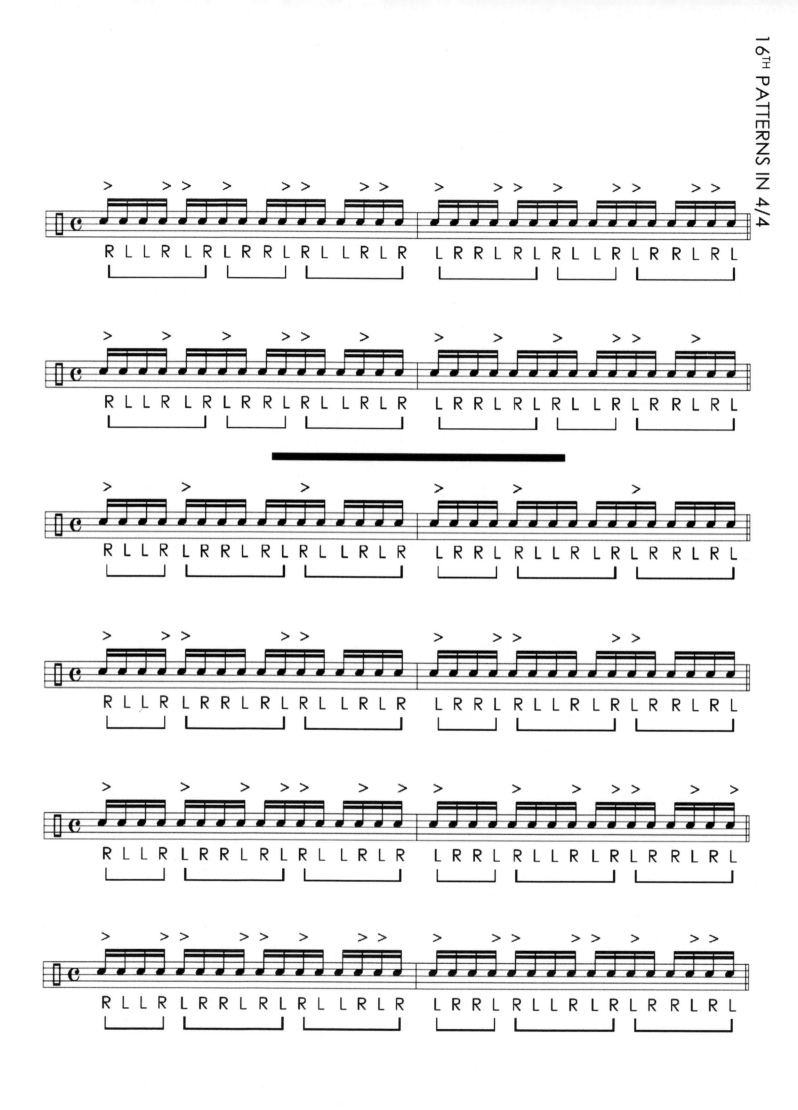

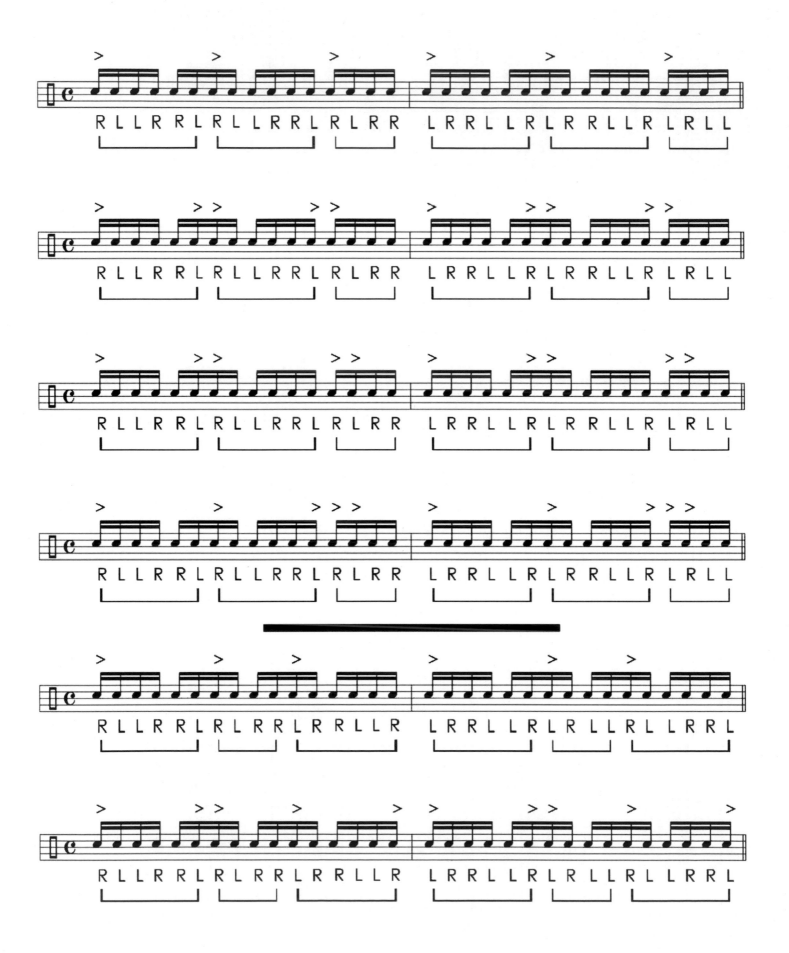

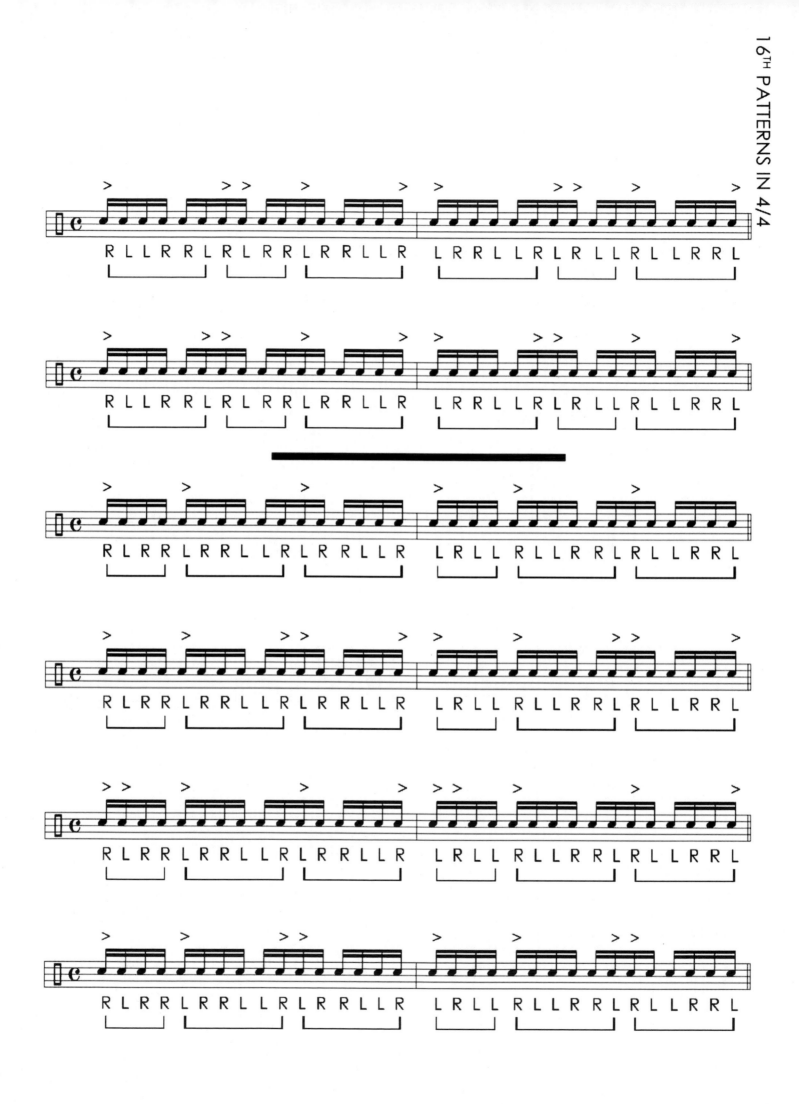

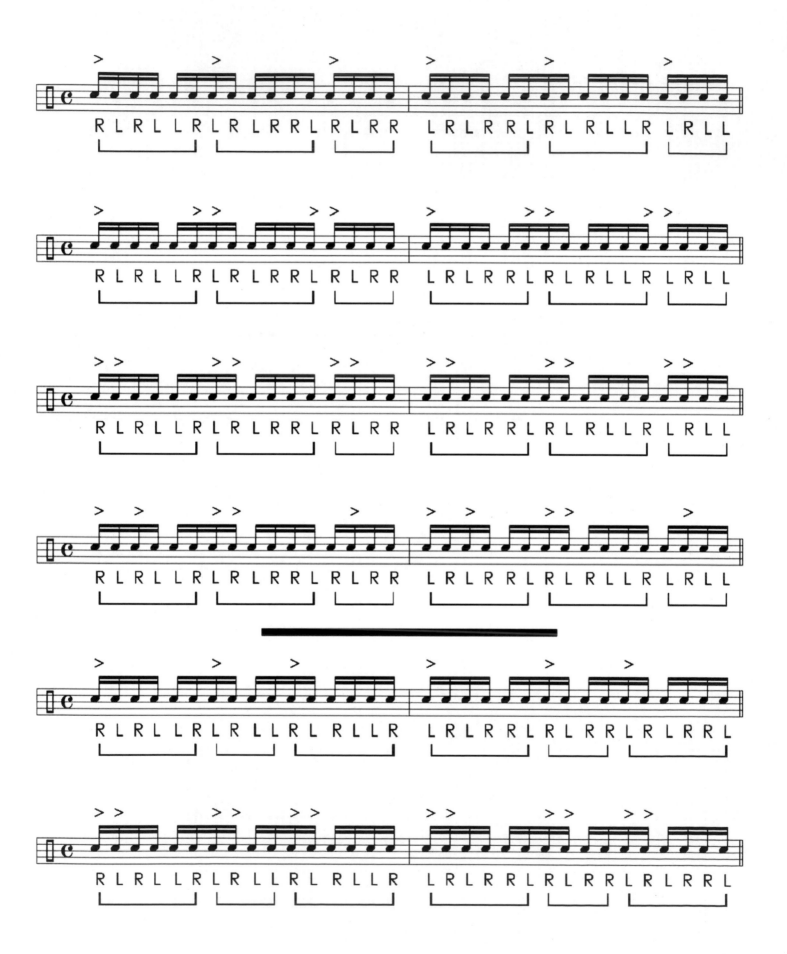

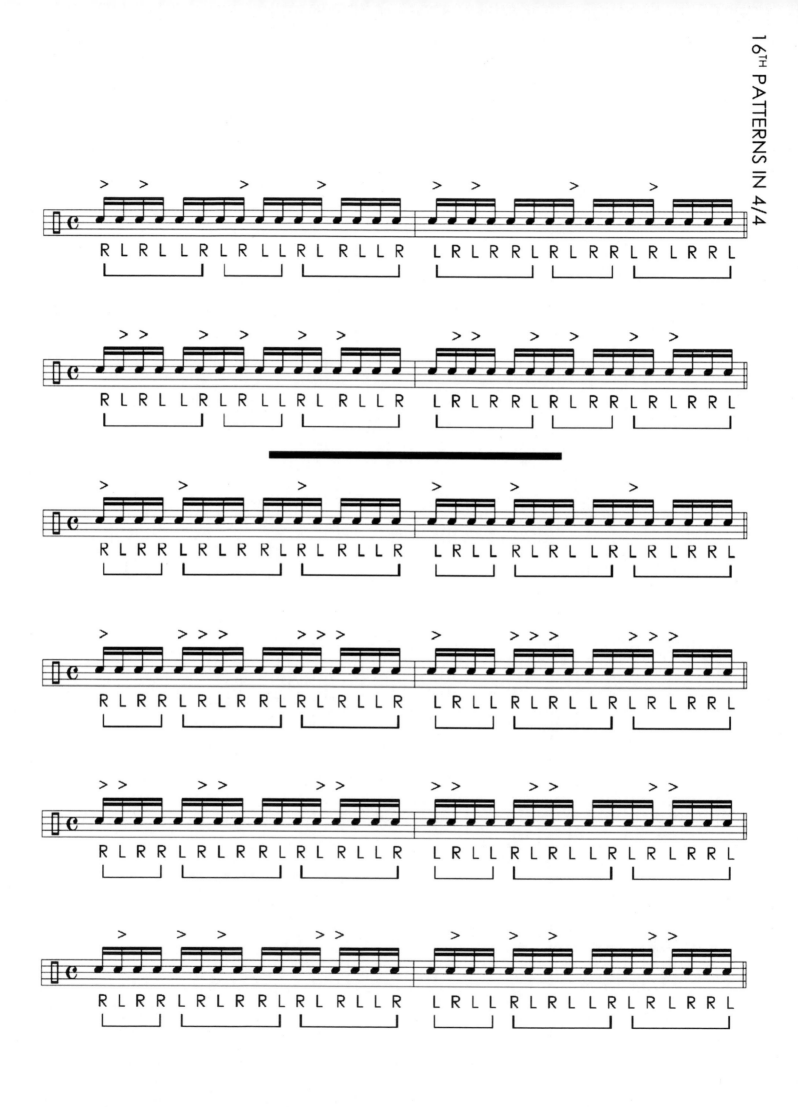

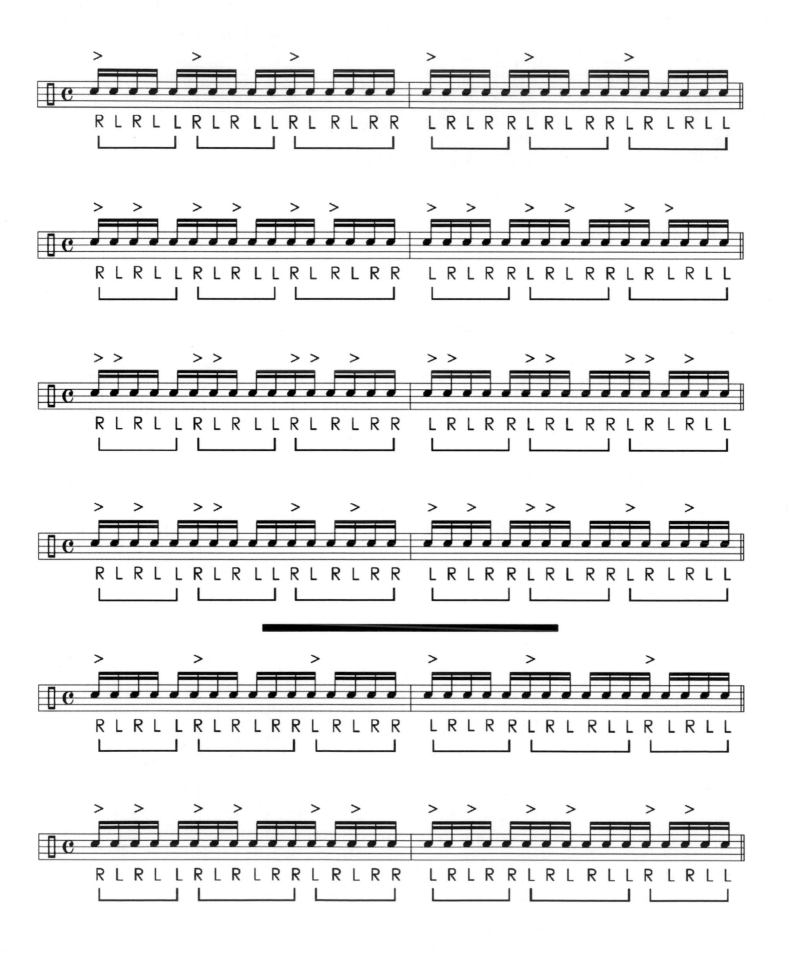

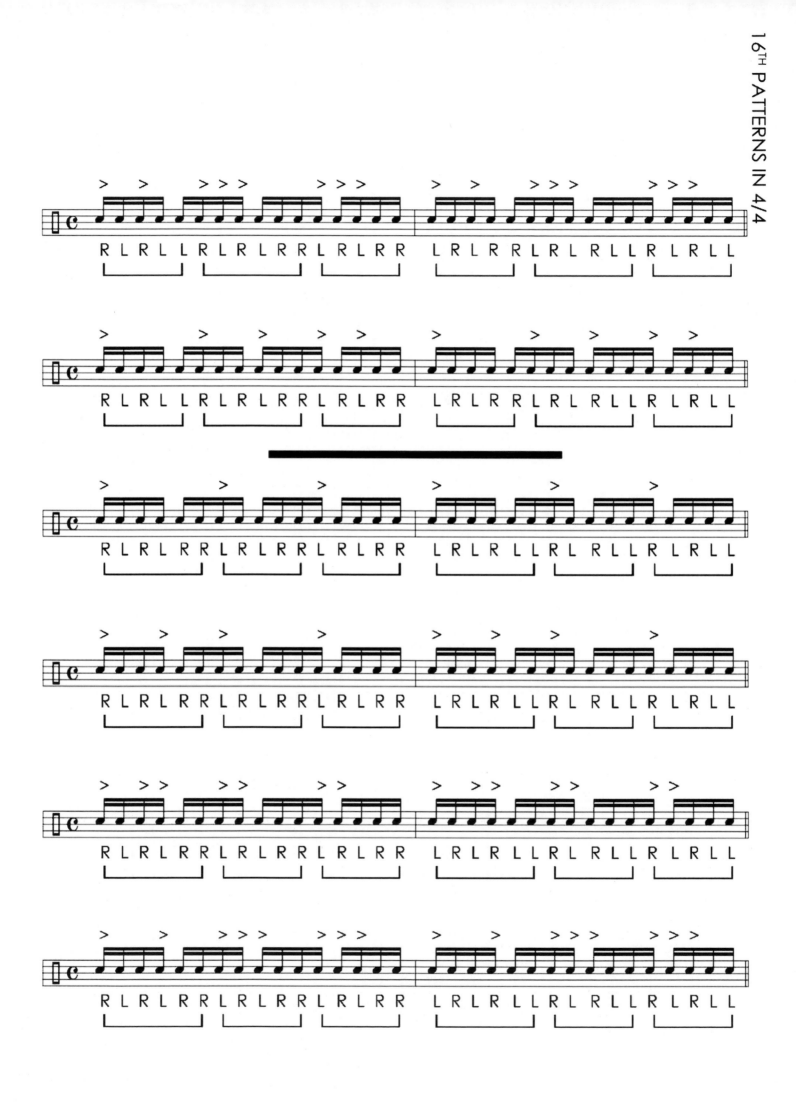

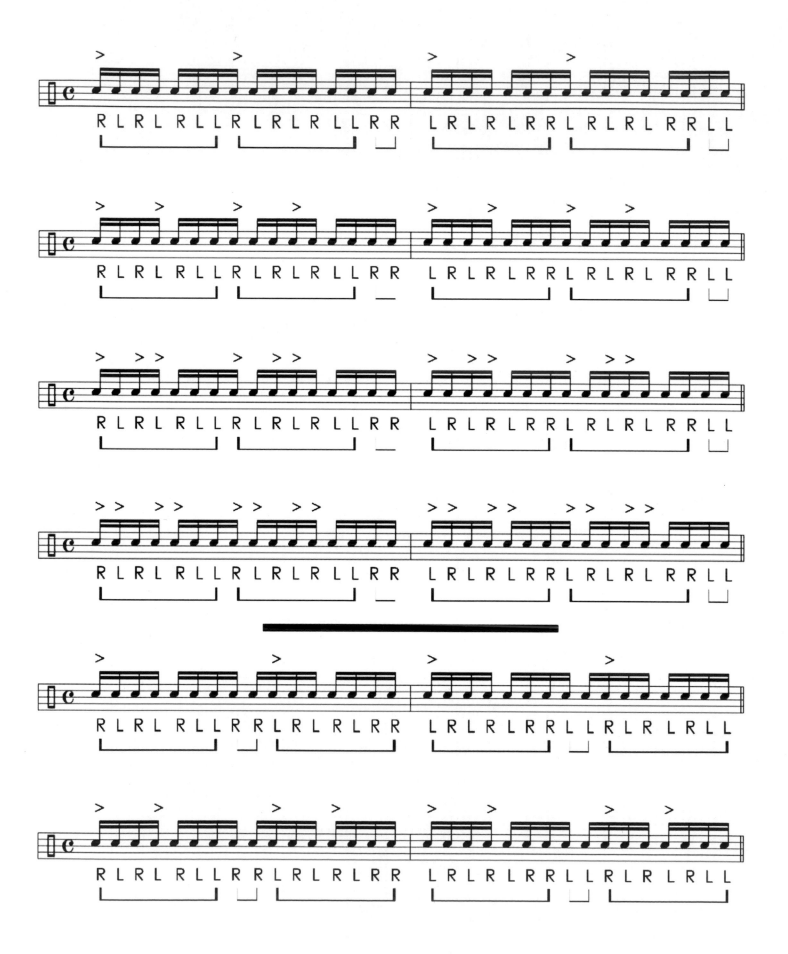

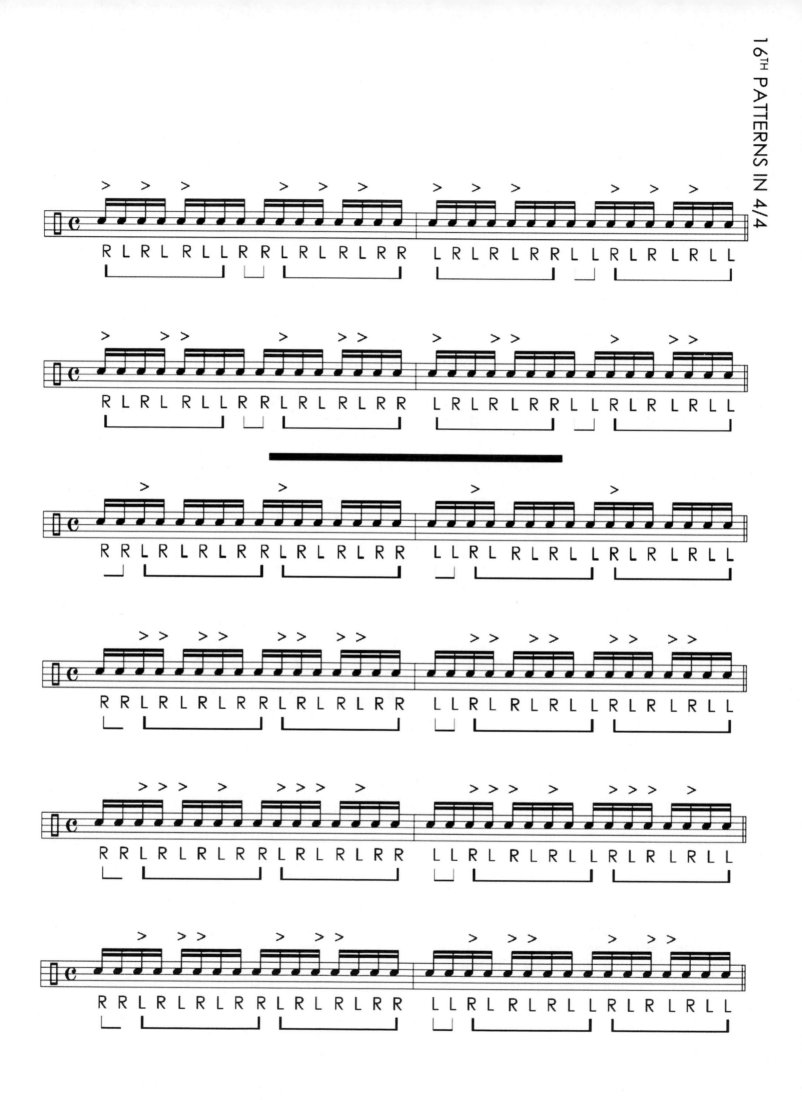

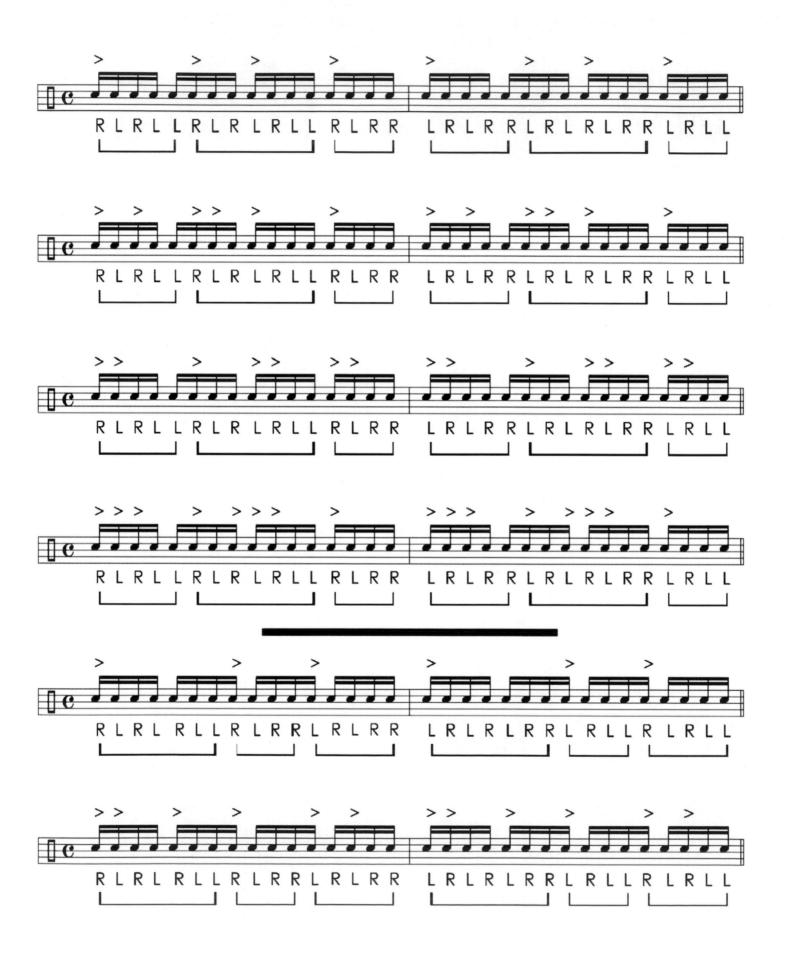

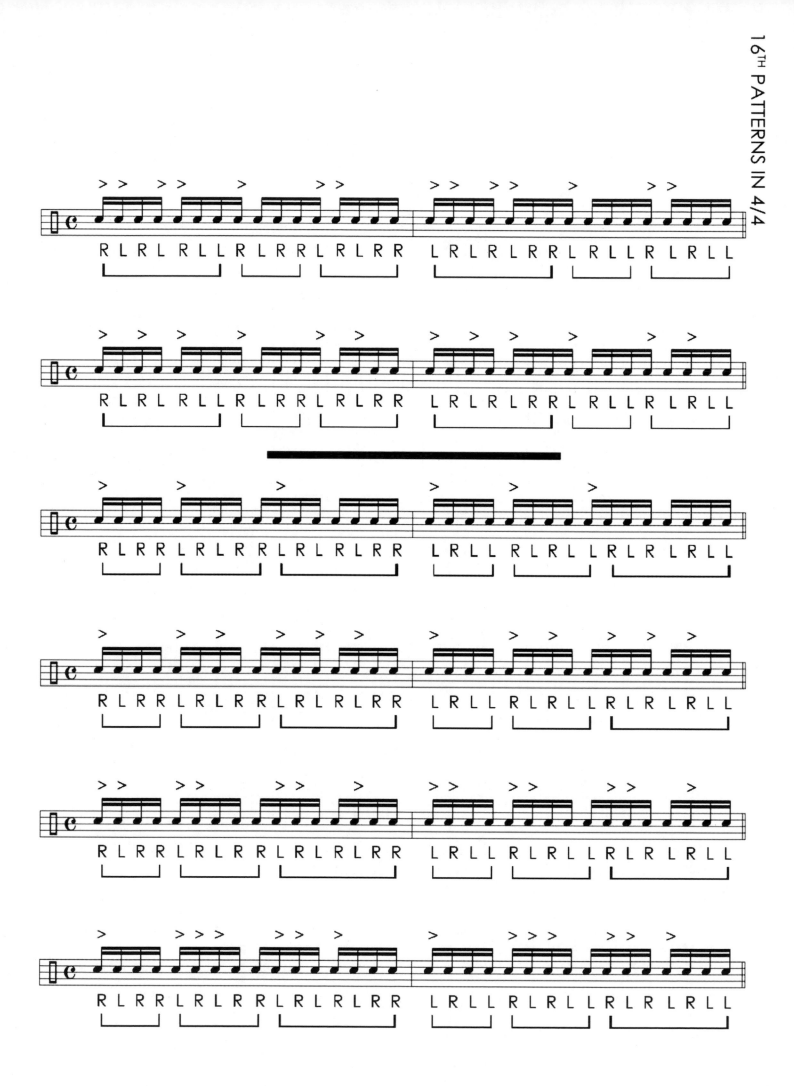

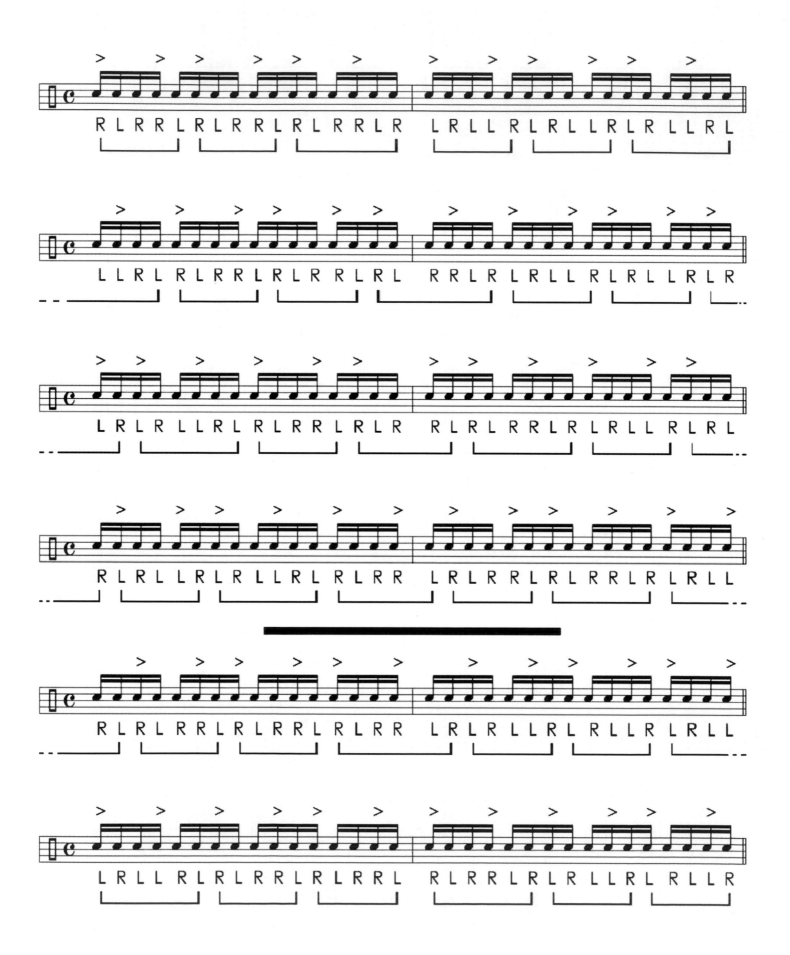

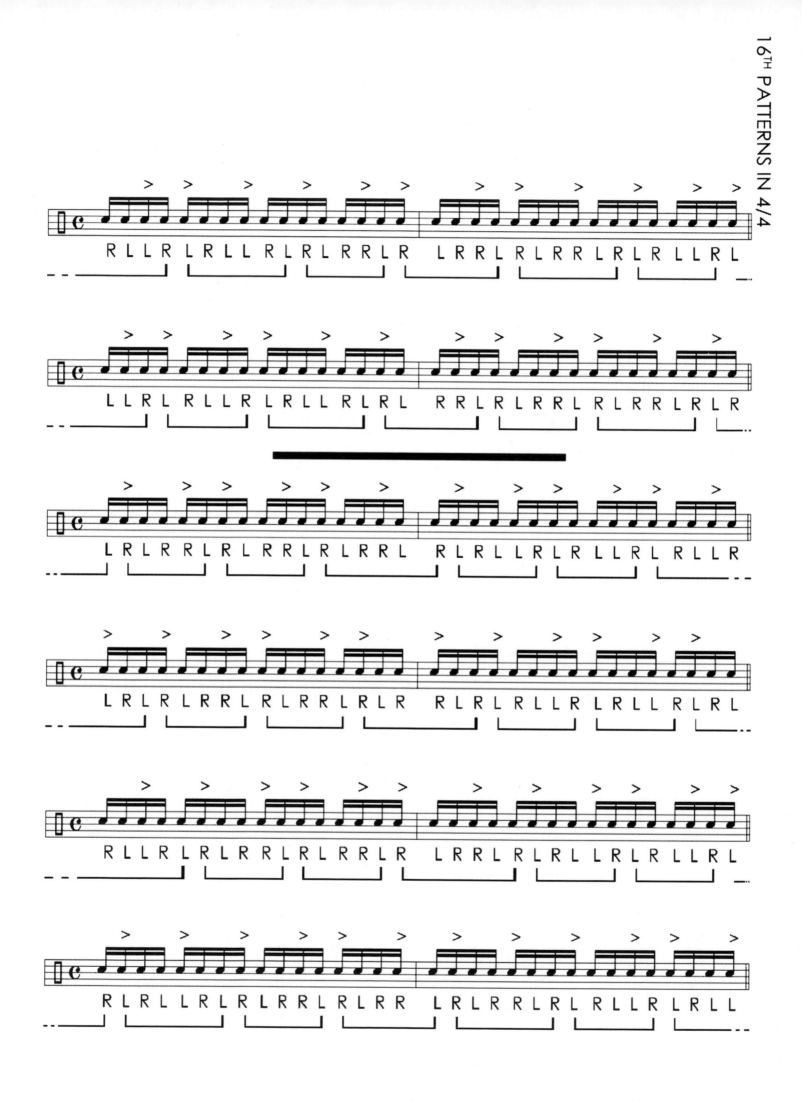

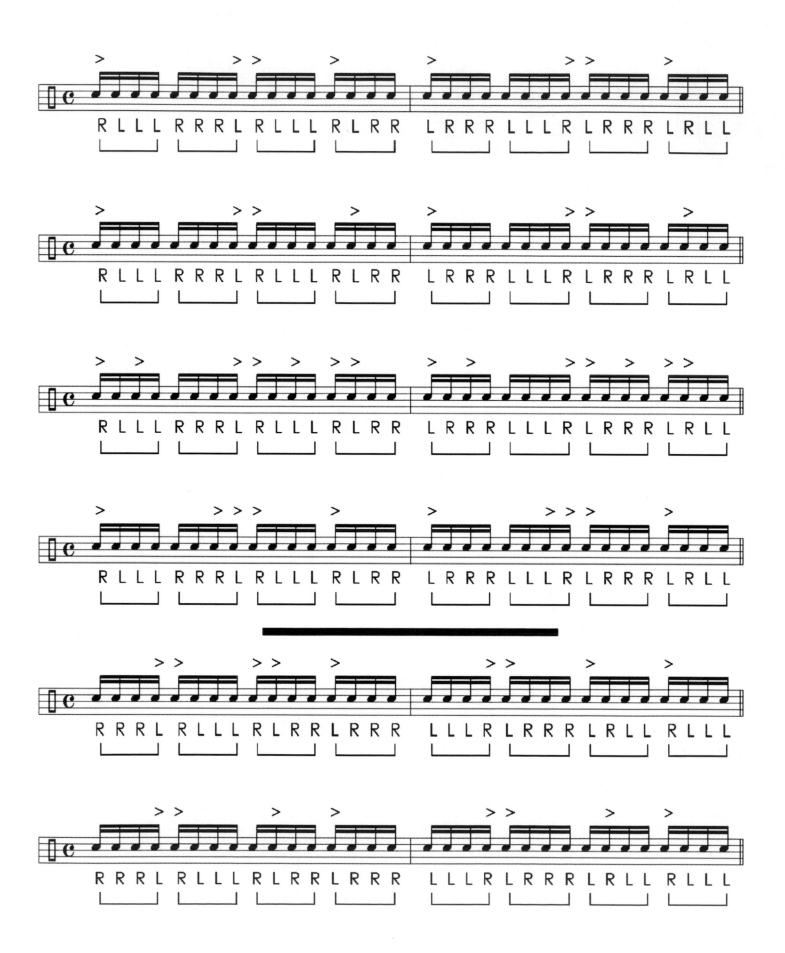

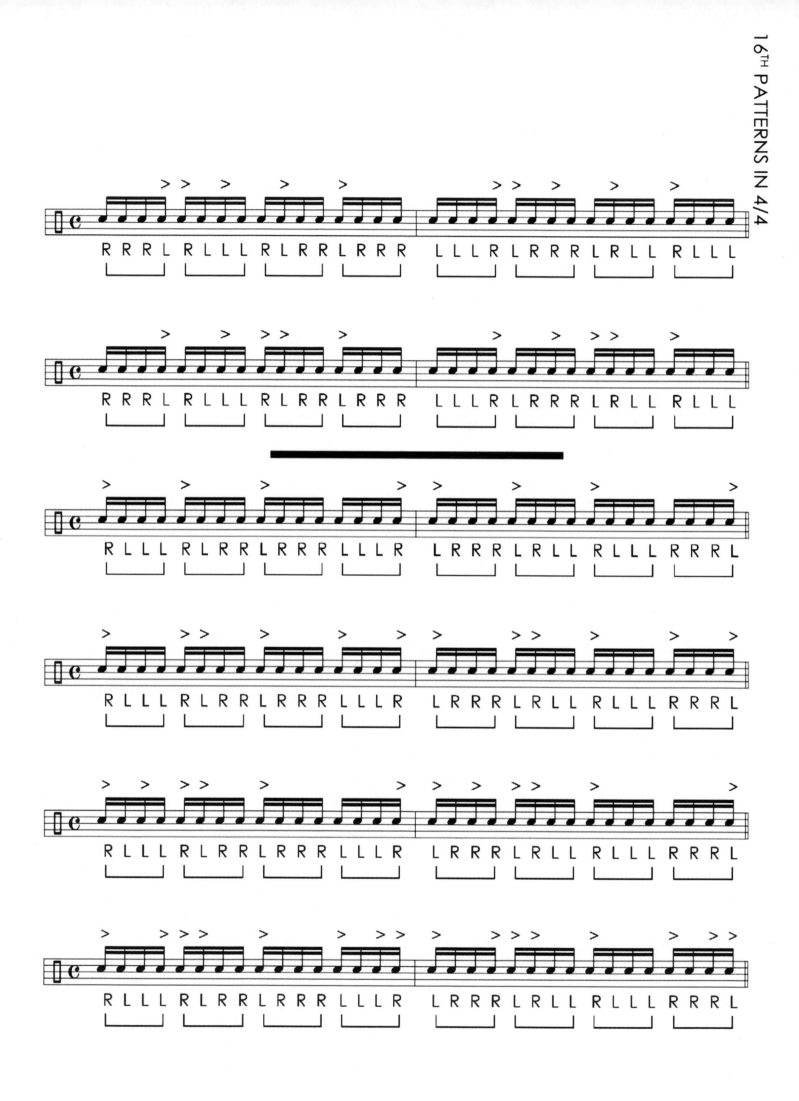

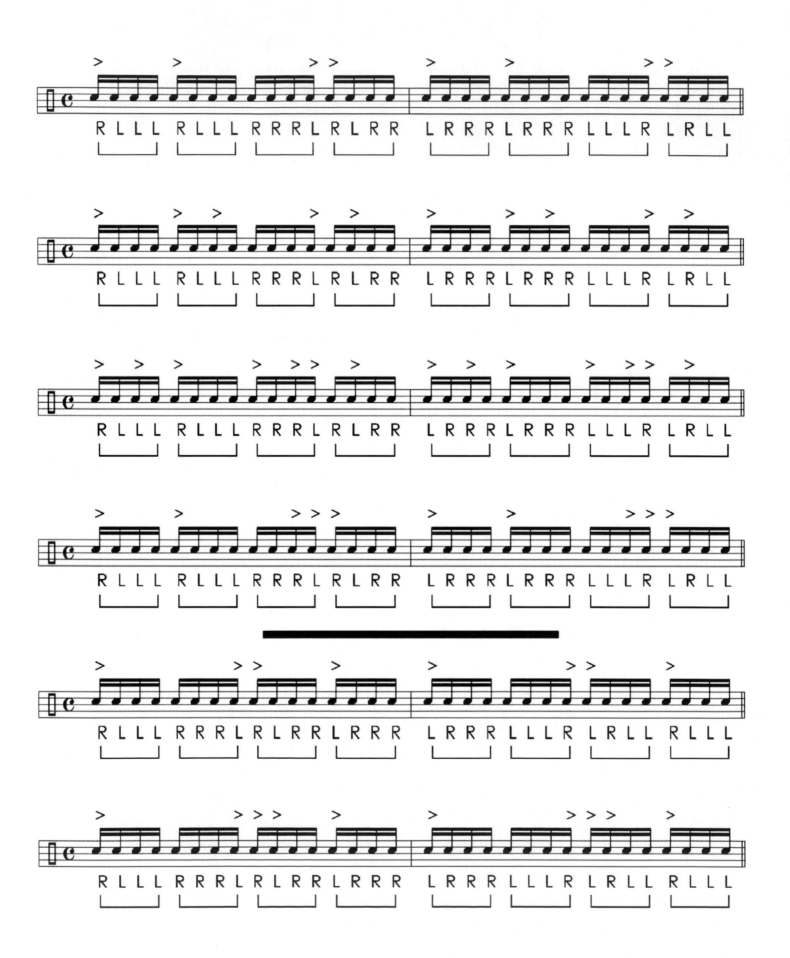

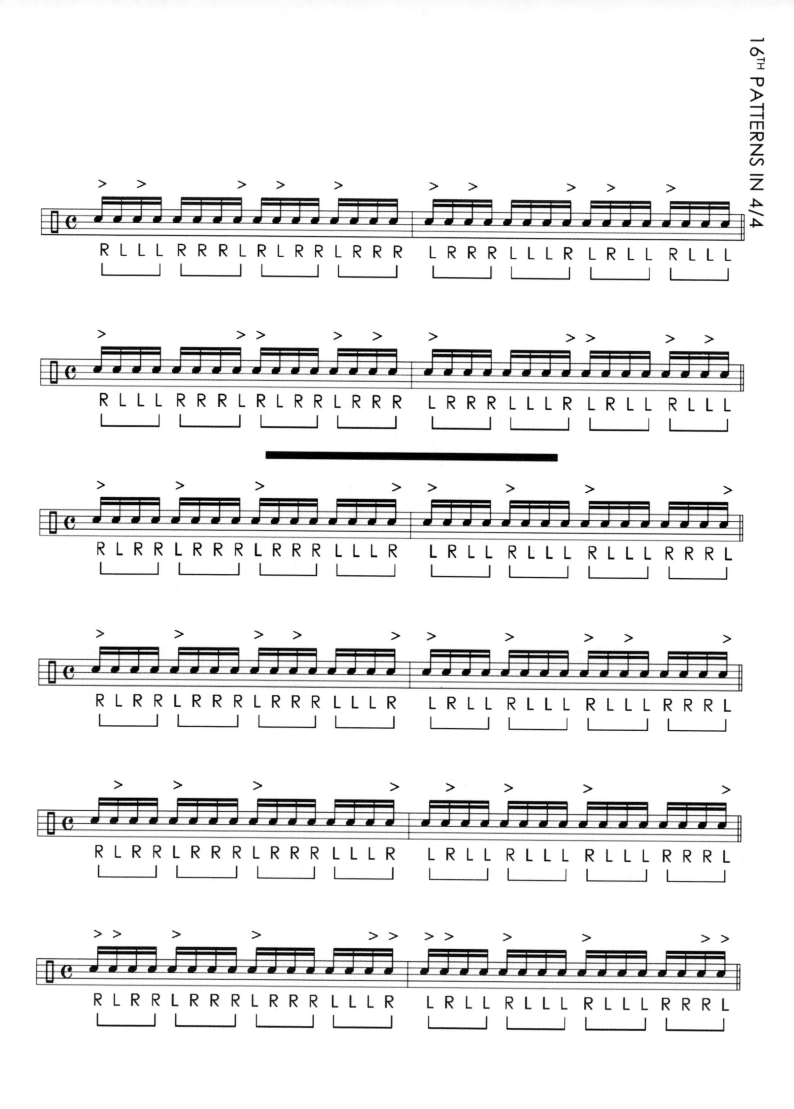

16th PATTERNS IN 6/8

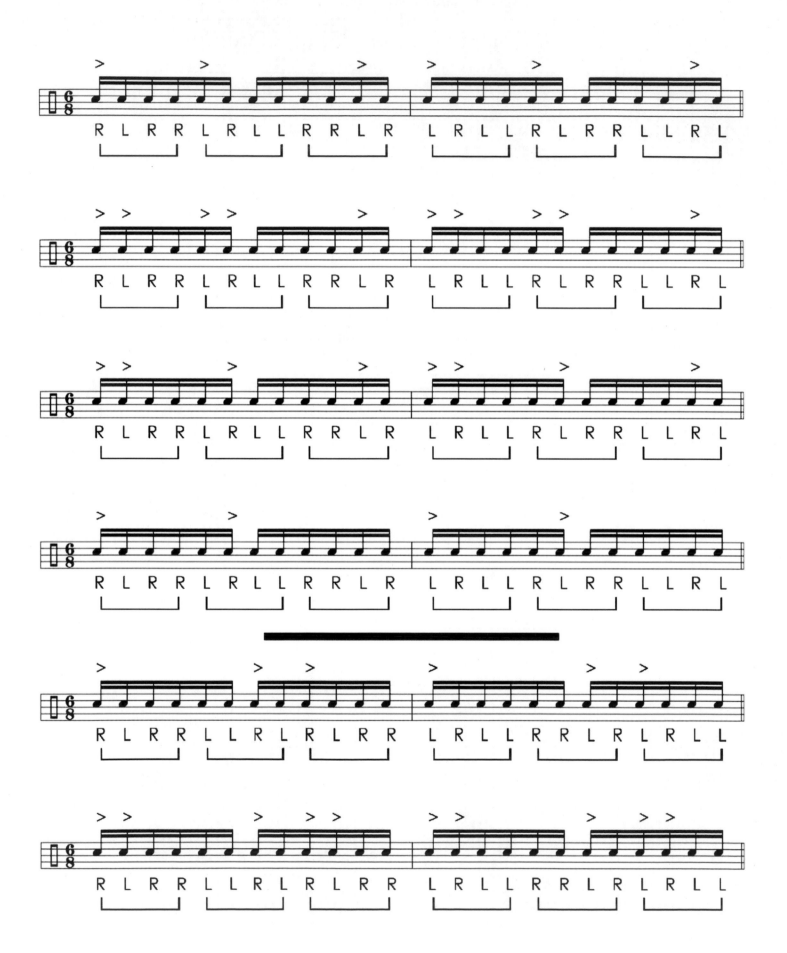

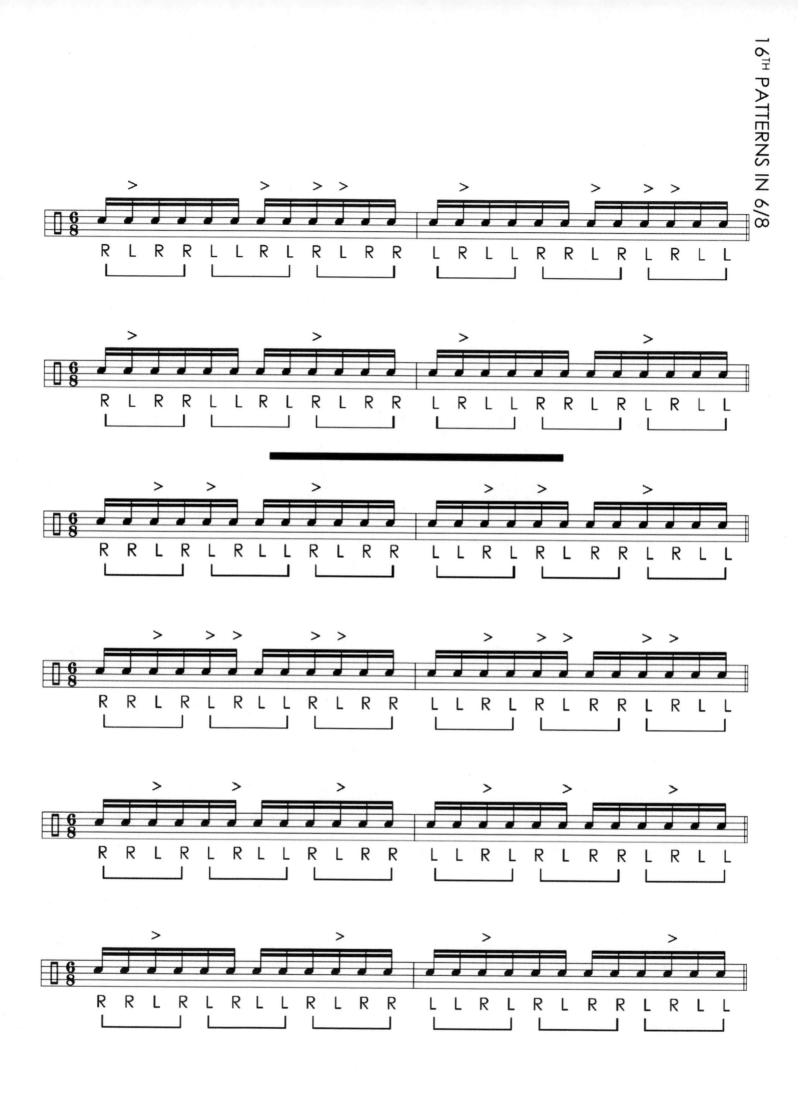

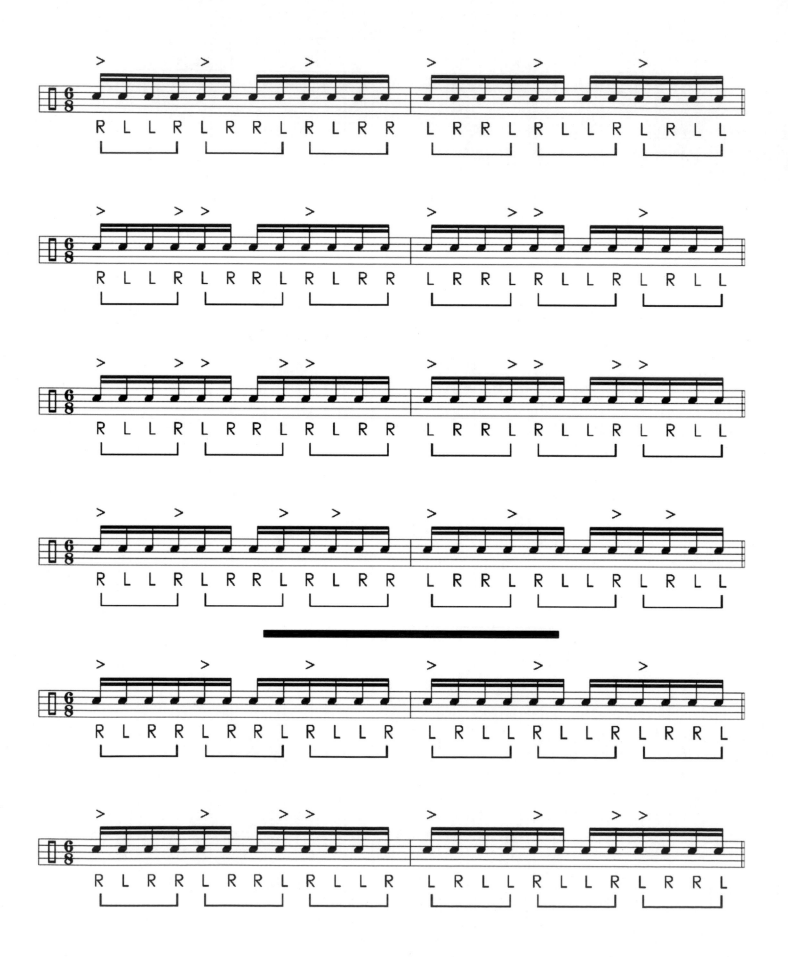

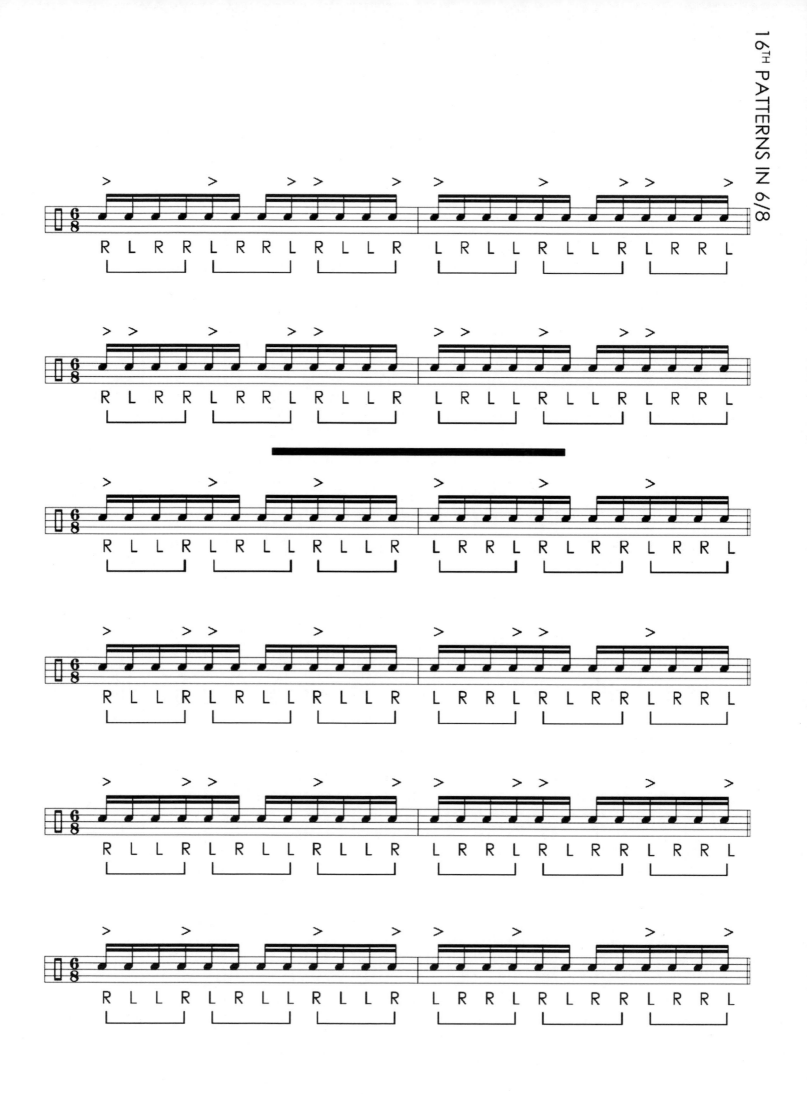

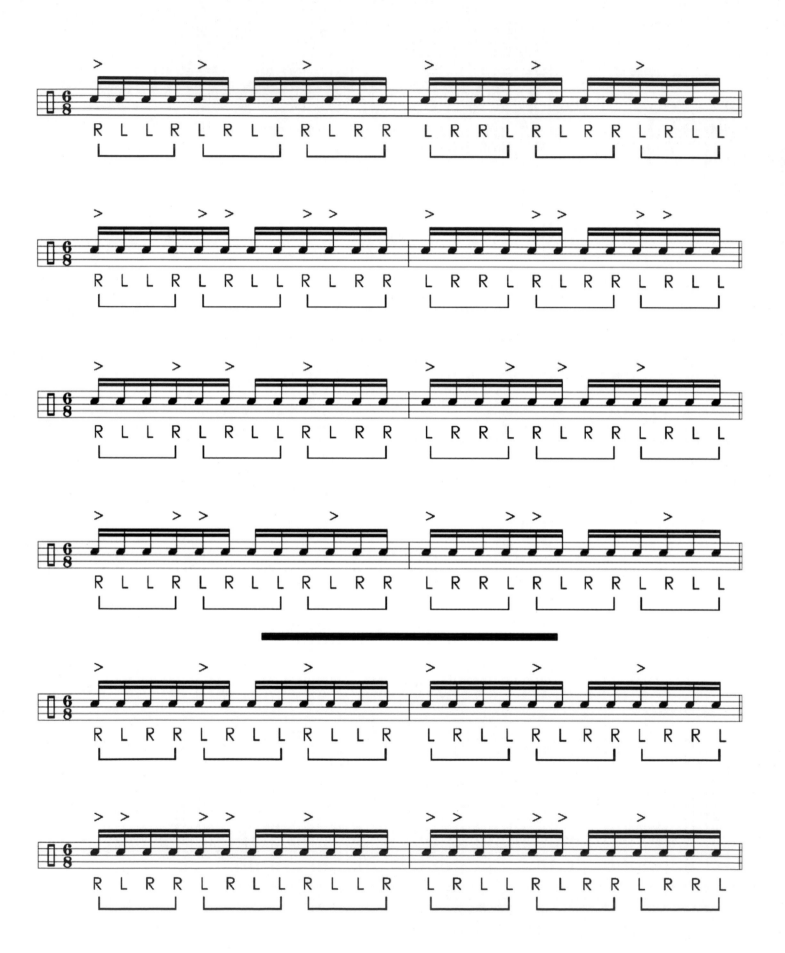

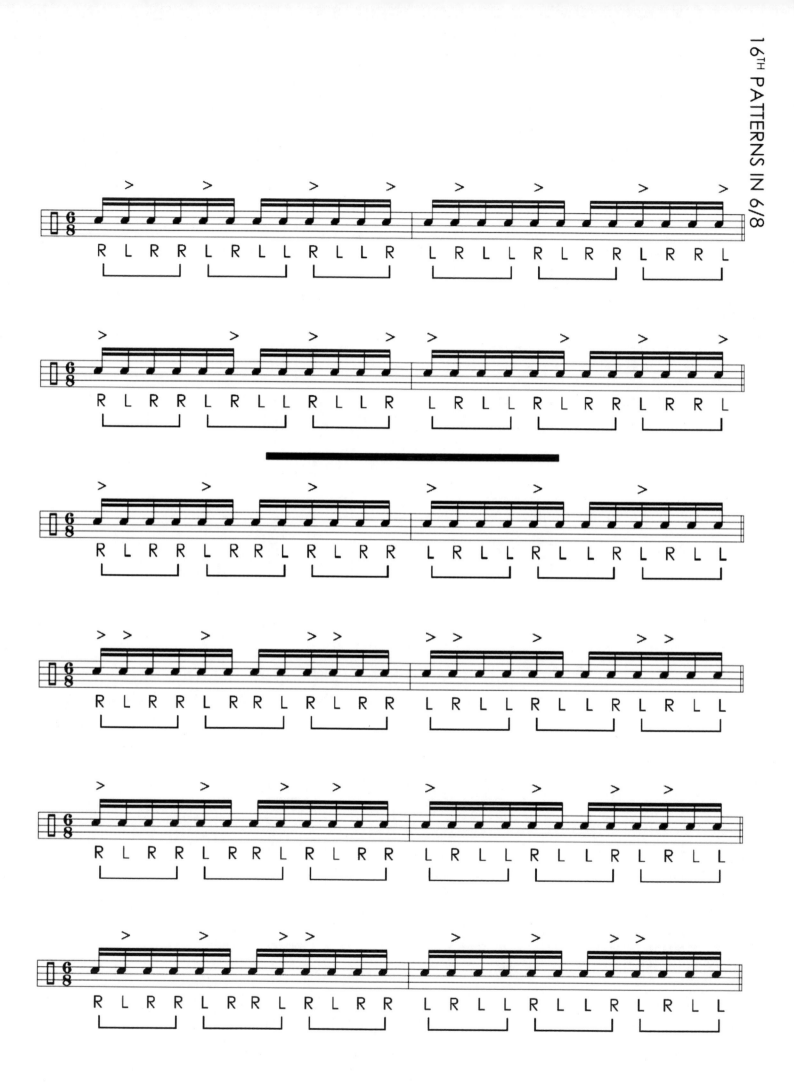

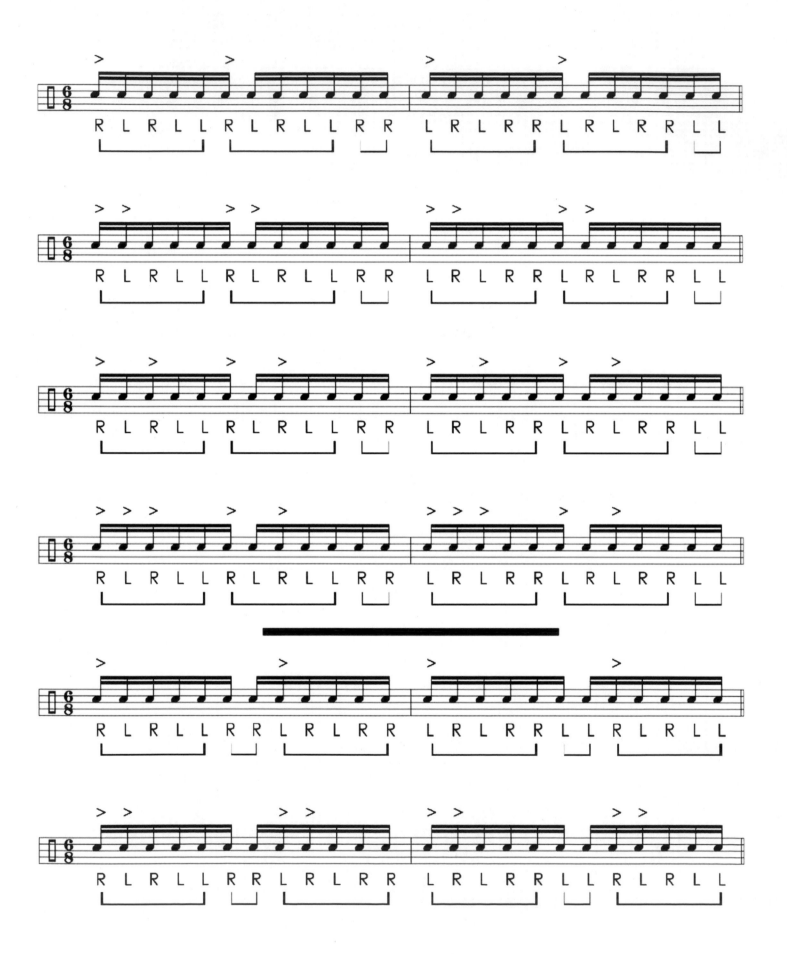

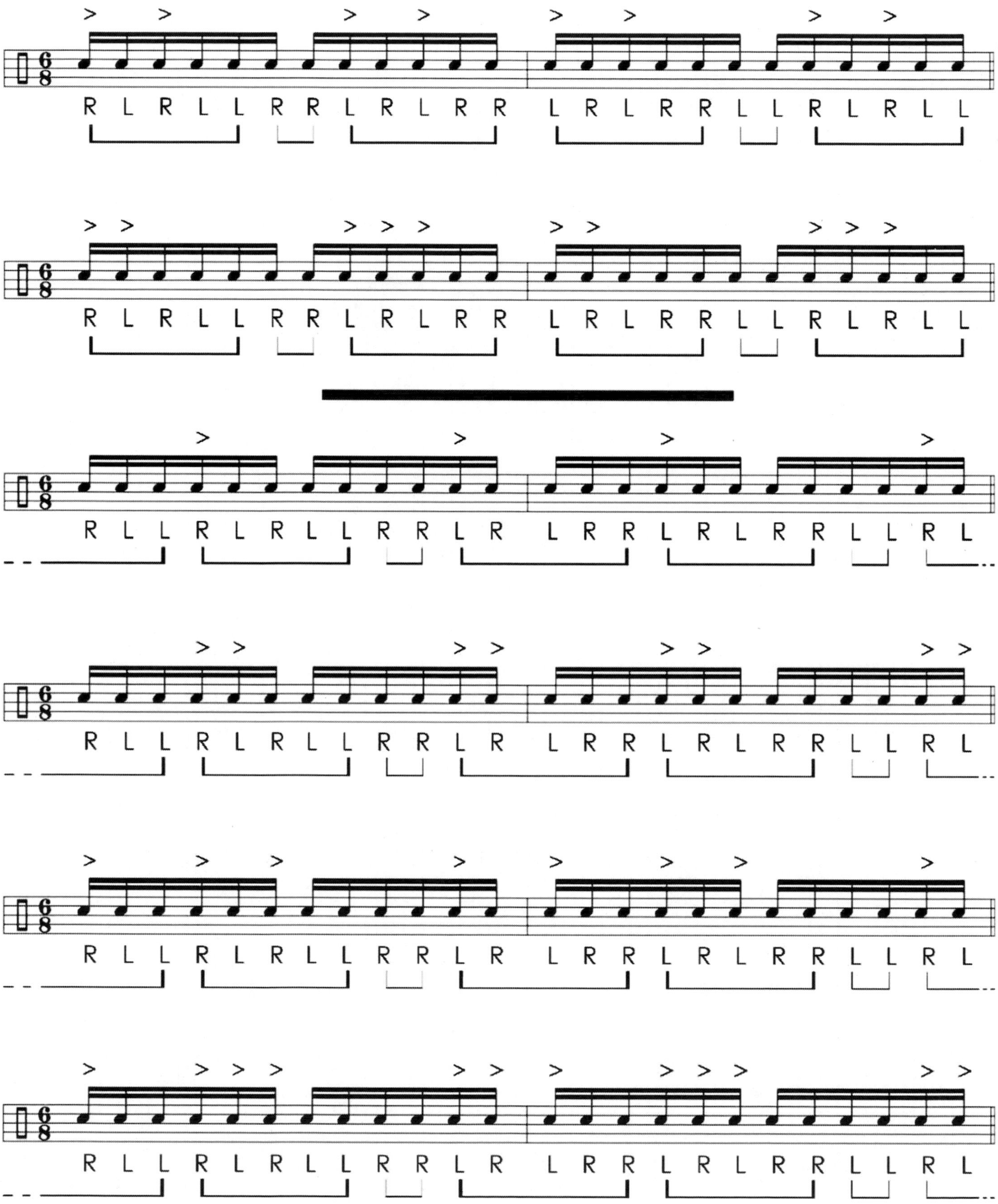

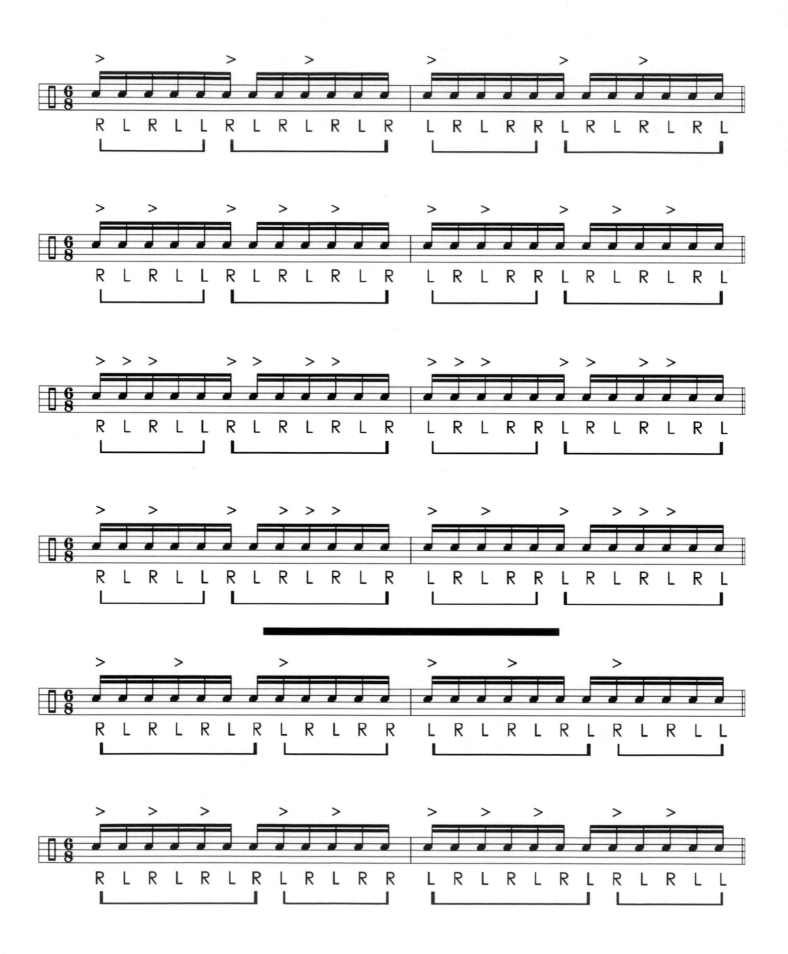

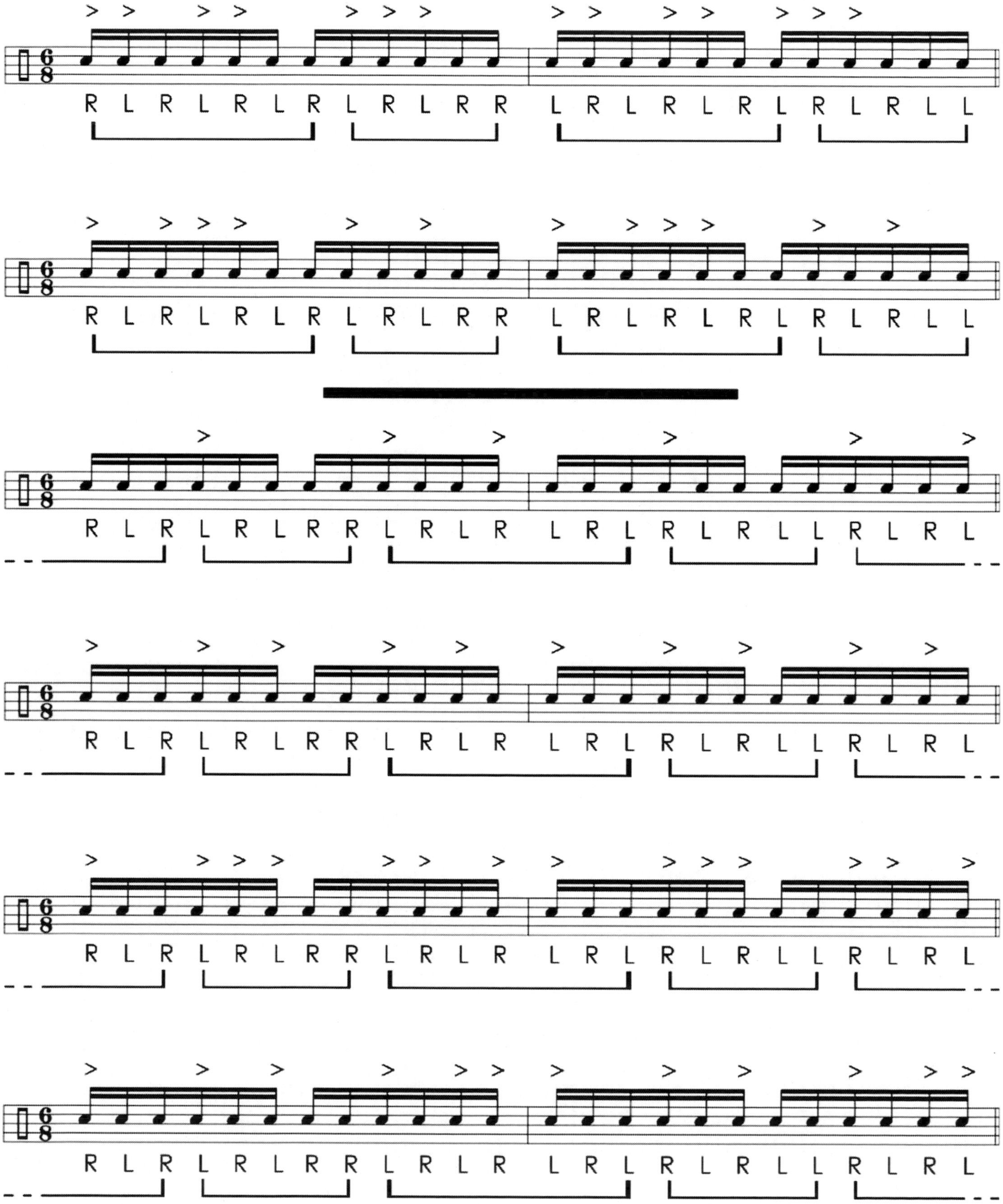
R L R L R L R L R L R R L R L R L R L R L R L L
R L R L R L R L R L R R L R L R L R L R L R L L
R L R L R L R R L R L R L R L R L R L L R L R L
R L R L R L R R L R L R L R L R L R L L R L R L
R L R L R L R R L R L R L R L R L R L L R L R L
R L R L R L R R L R L R L R L R L R L L R L R L

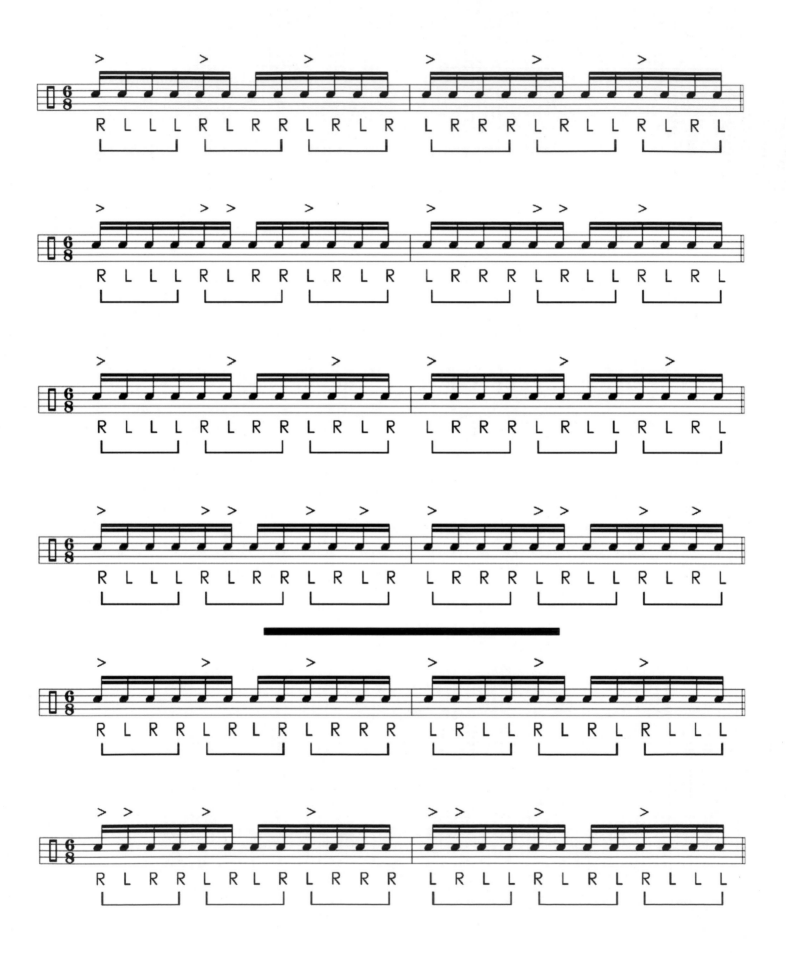

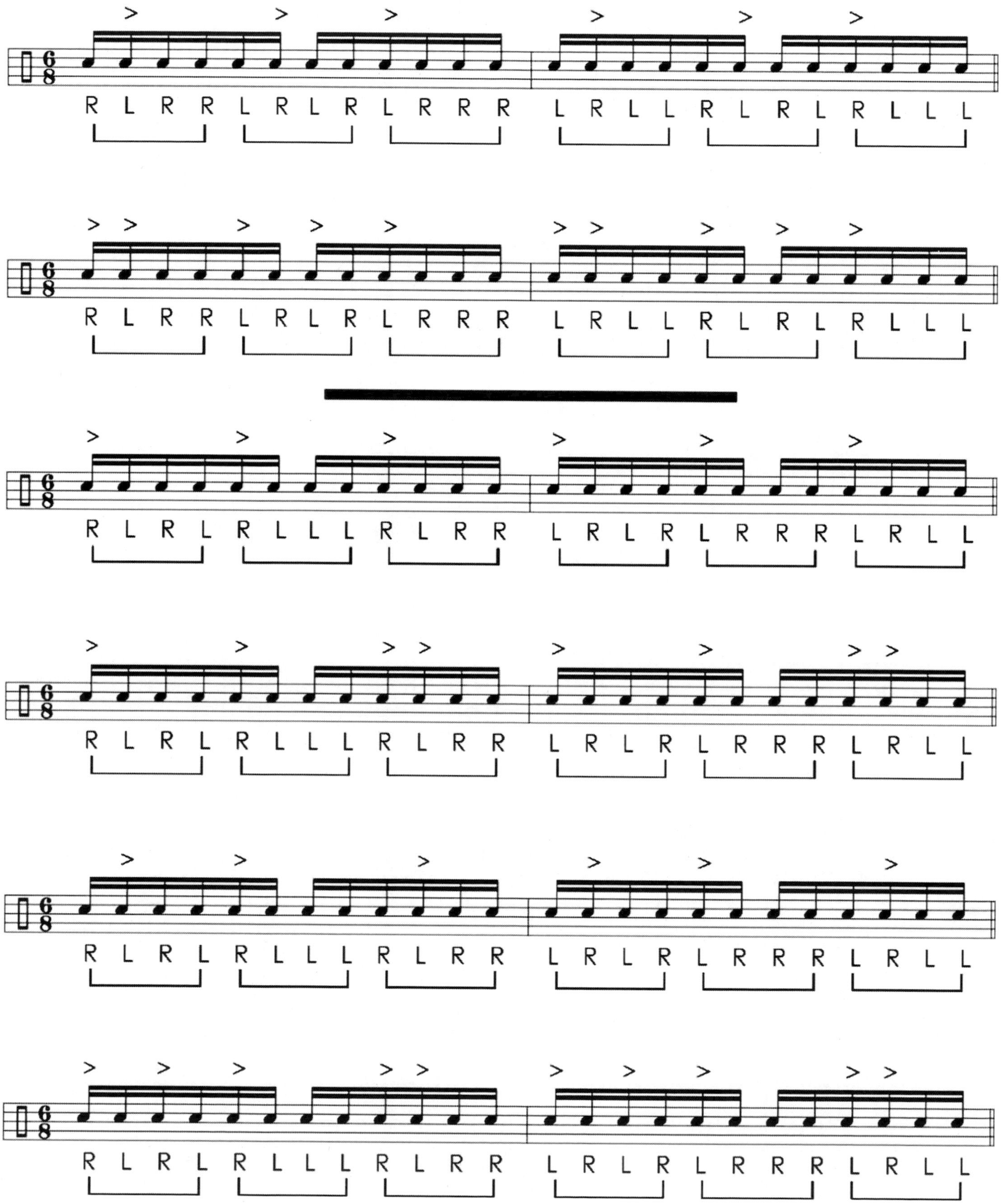
R L R R L R L R L R R R L R L L R L R L R L L L
R L R R L R L R L R R R L R L L R L R L R L L L
R L R L R L L L R L R R L R L R L R R R L R L L
R L R L R L L L R L R R L R L R L R R R L R L L
R L R L R L L L R L R R L R L R L R R R L R L L
R L R L R L L L R L R R L R L R L R R R L R L L

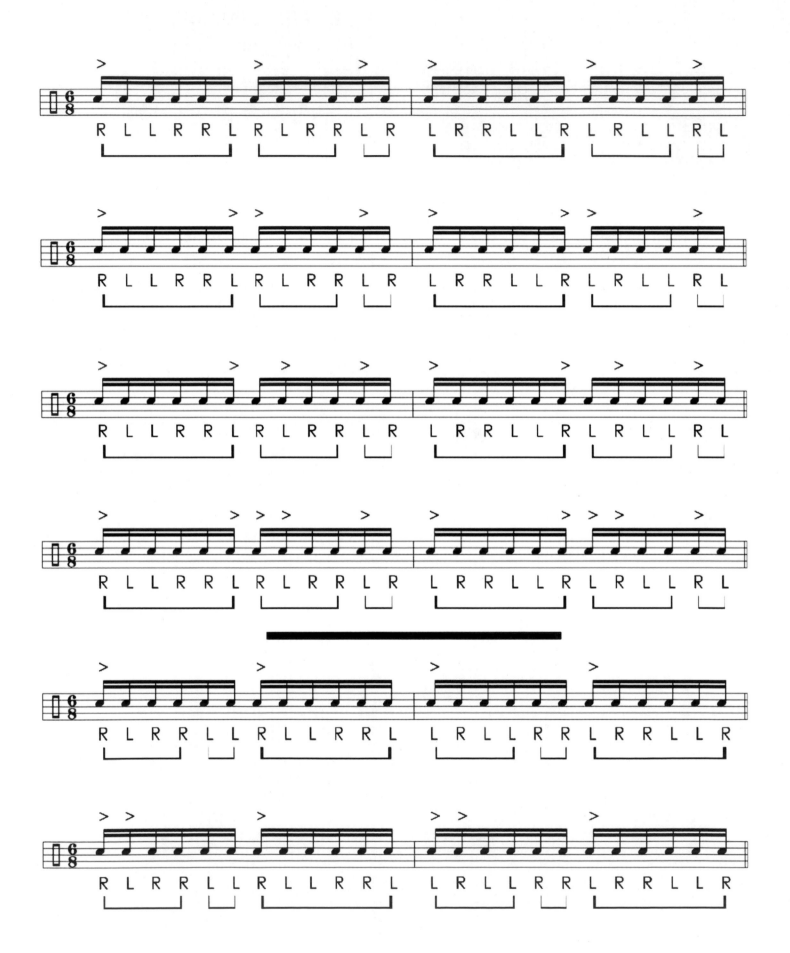

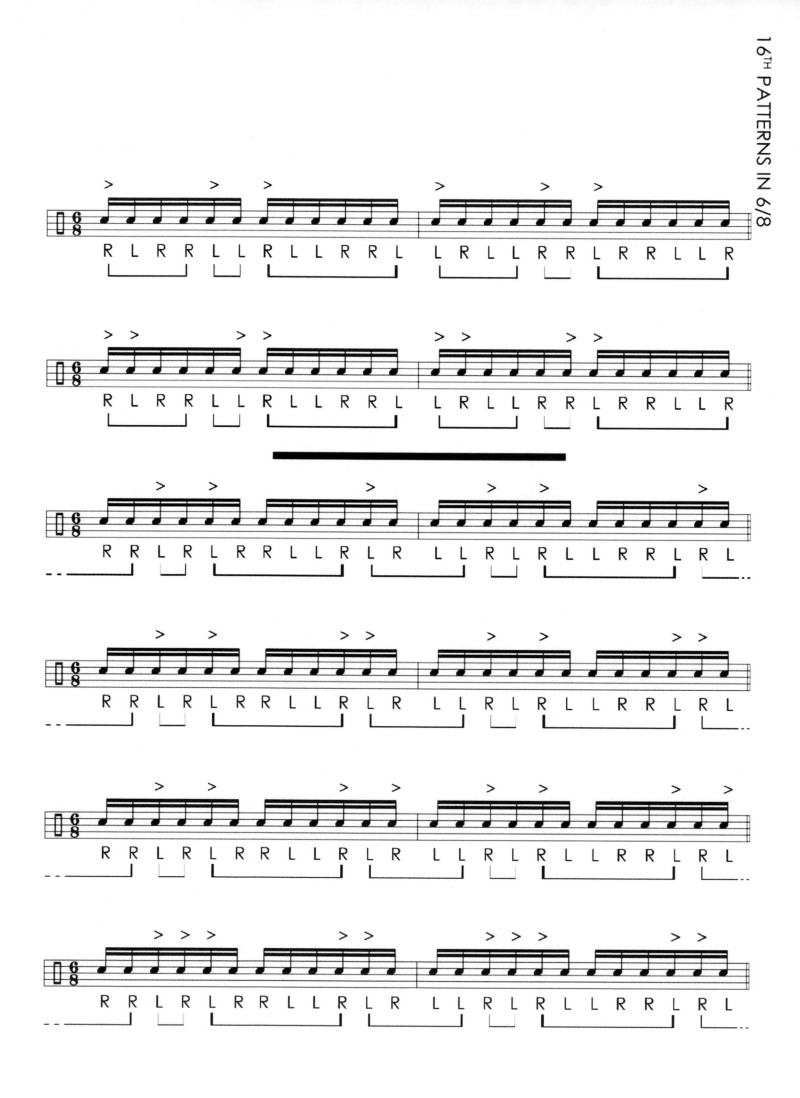

16ᵗʰ PATTERNS IN 5/4

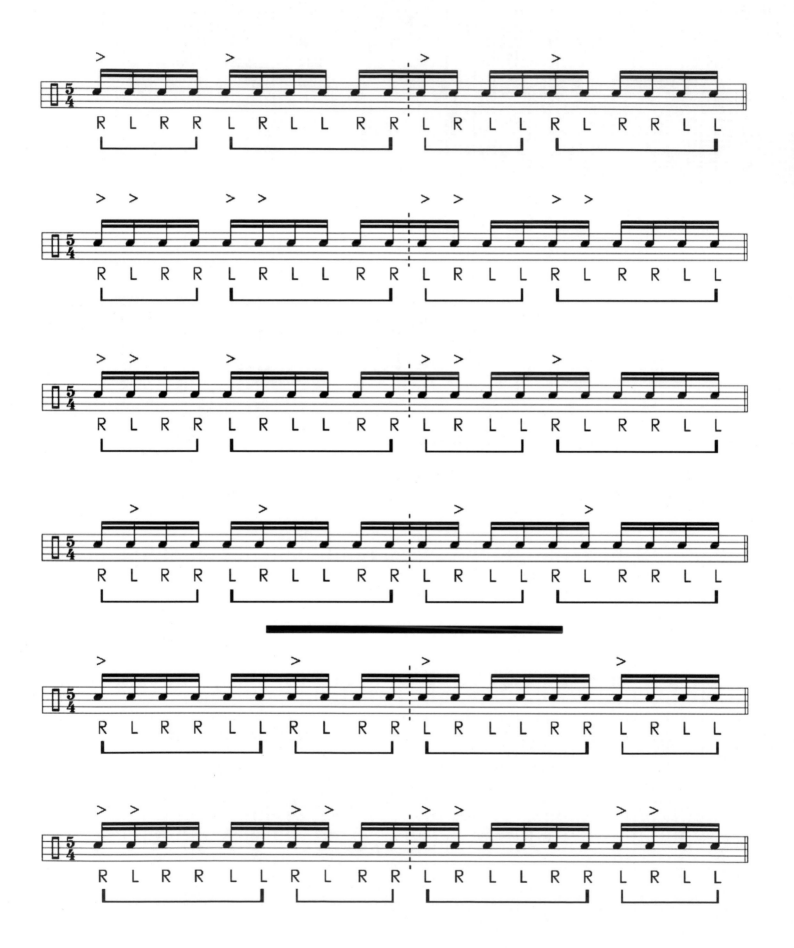

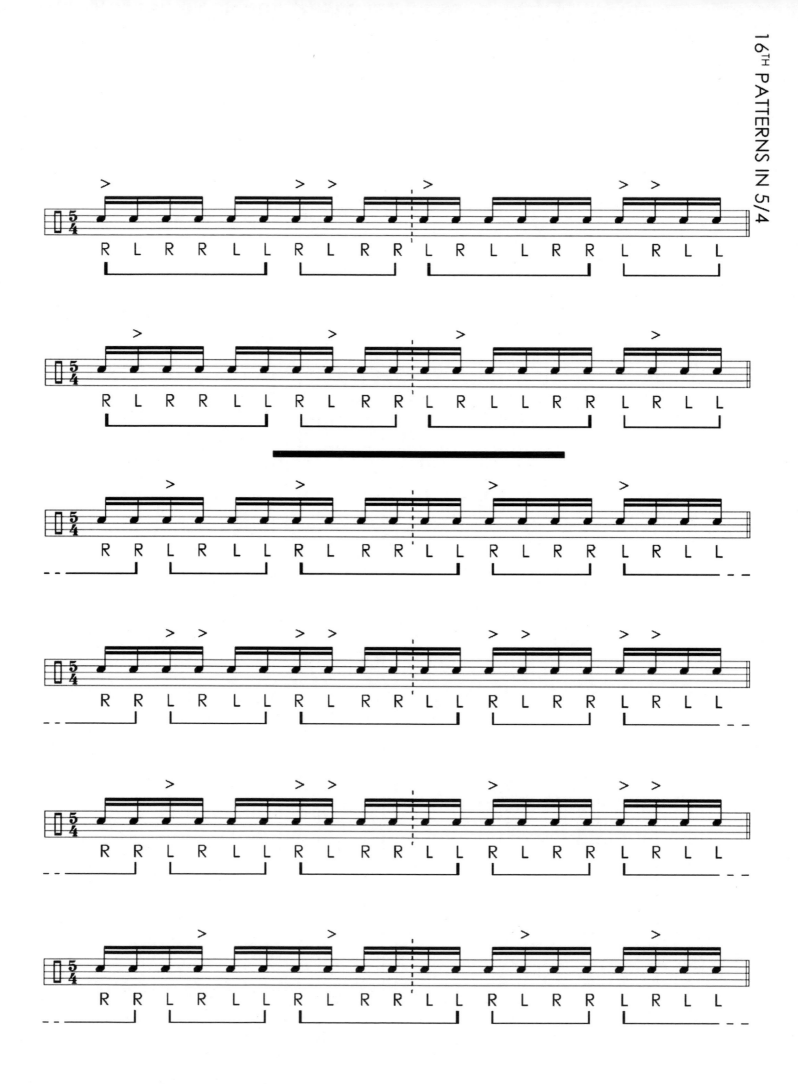

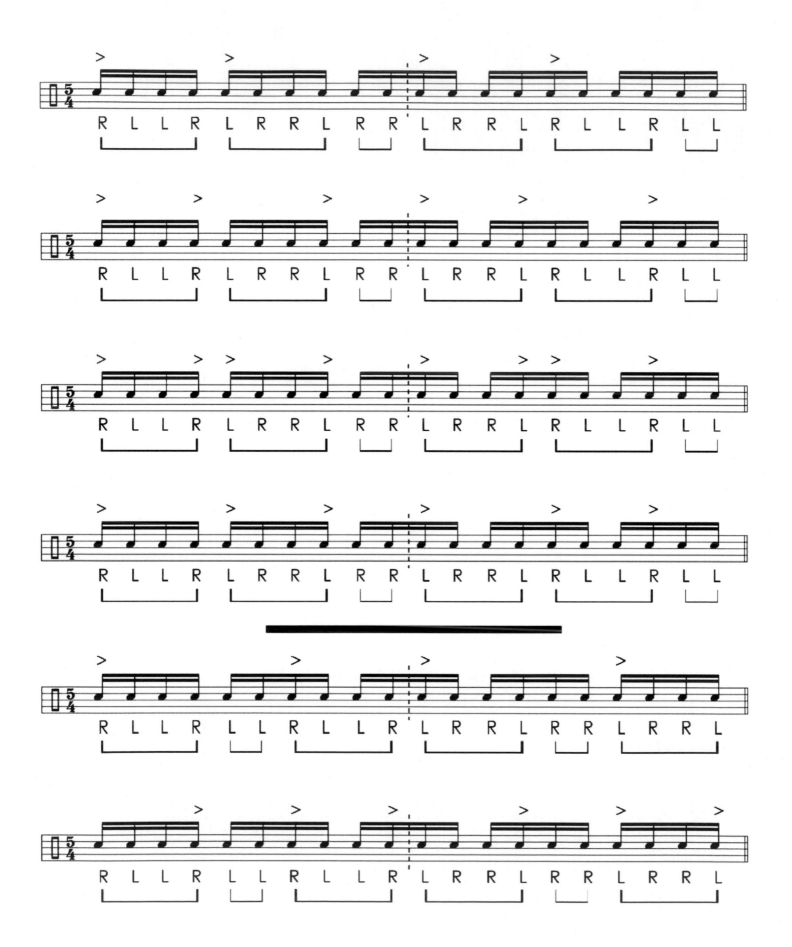

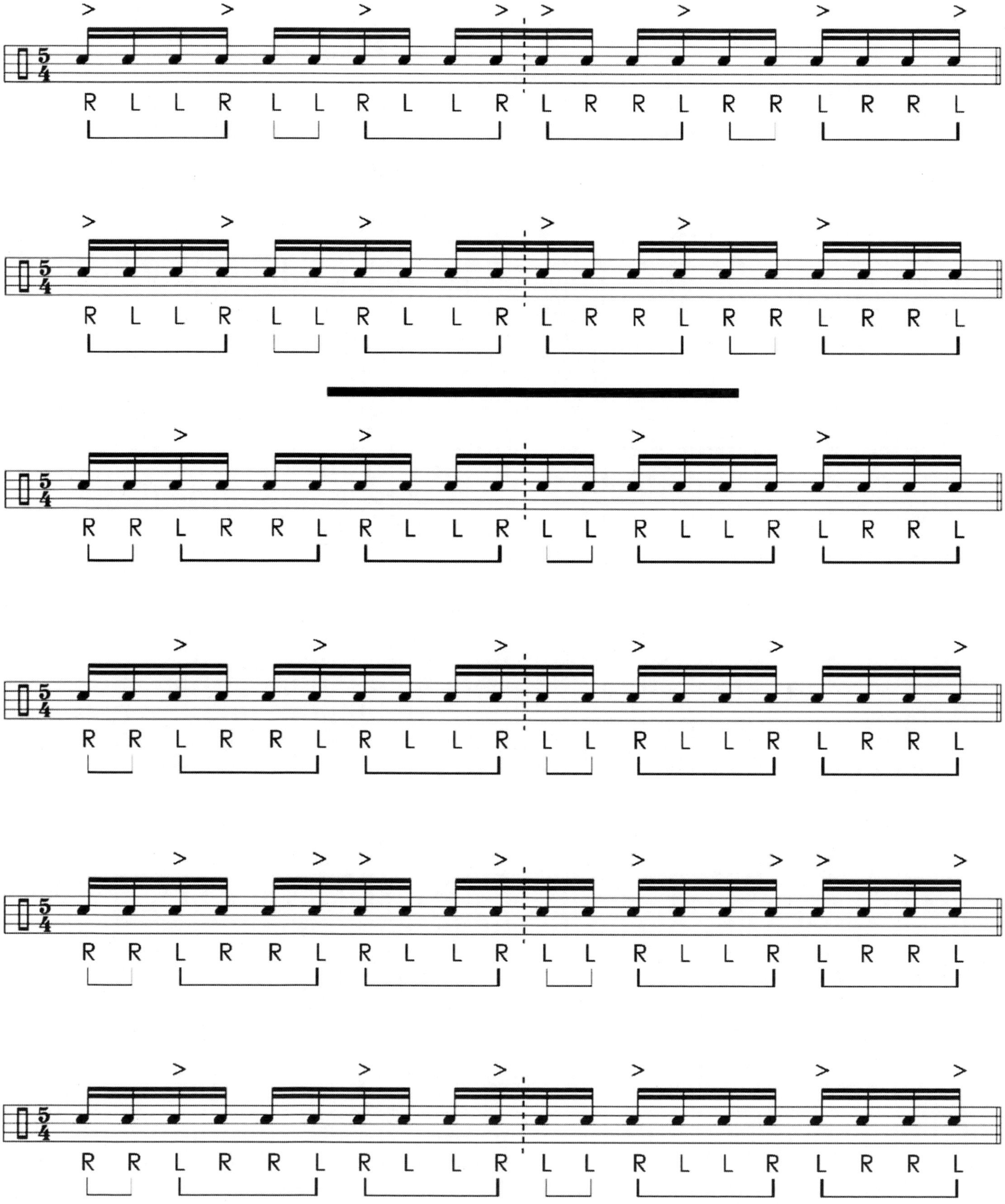

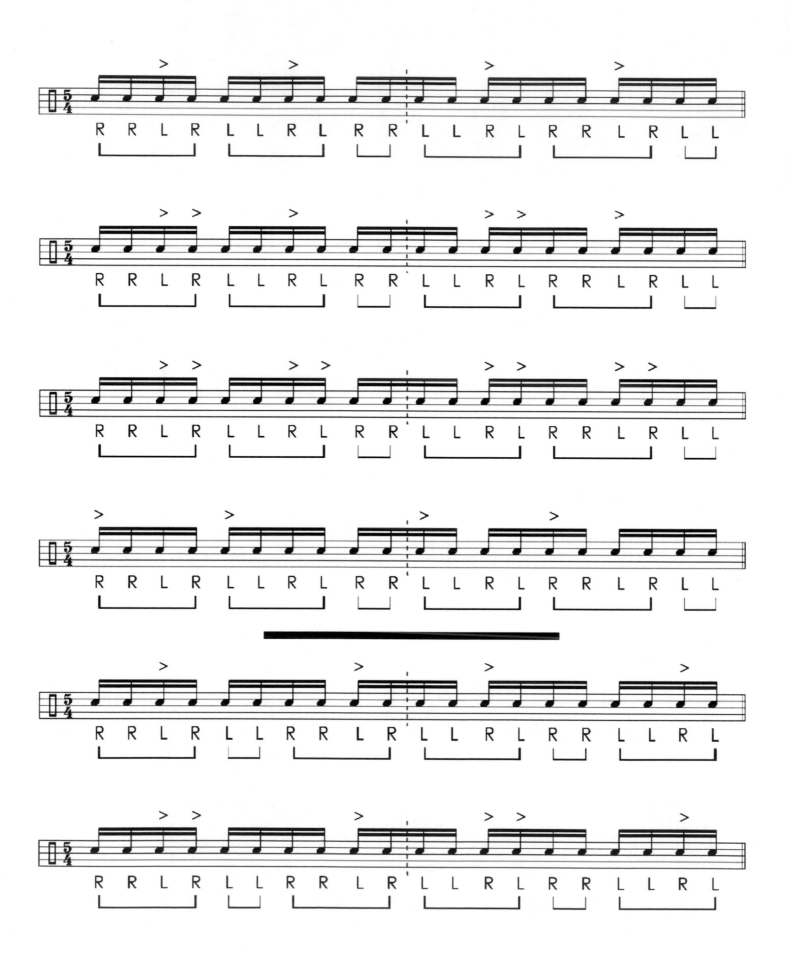

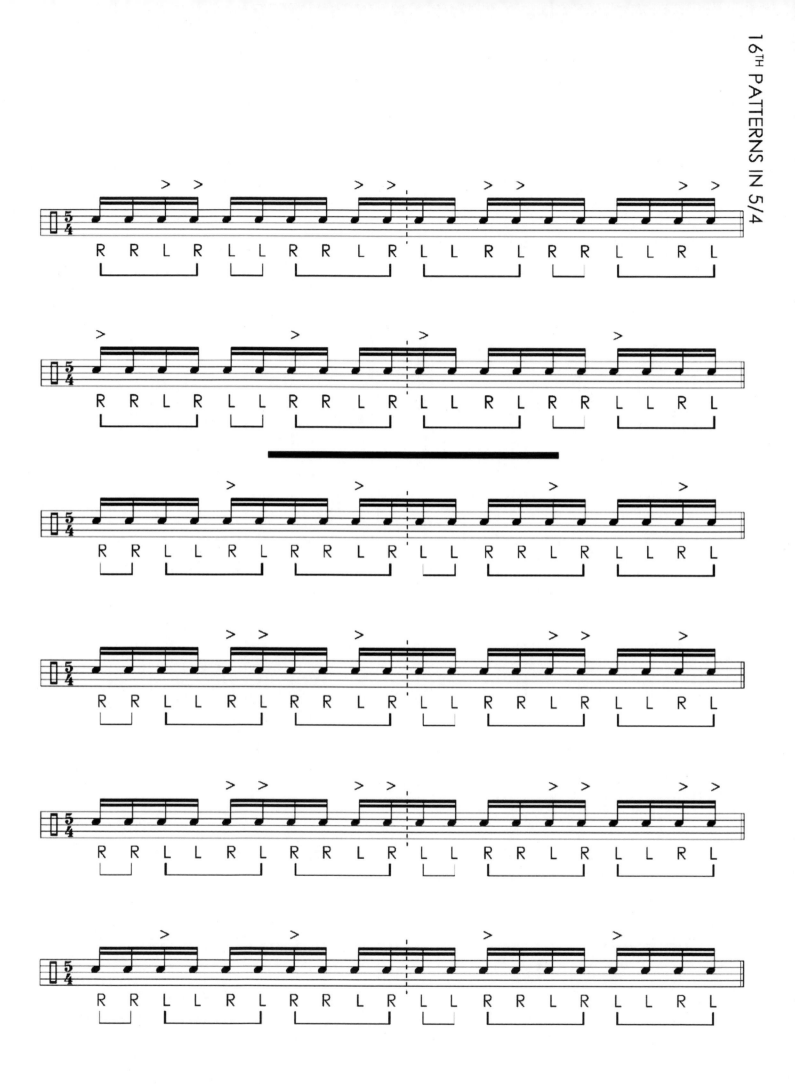

46

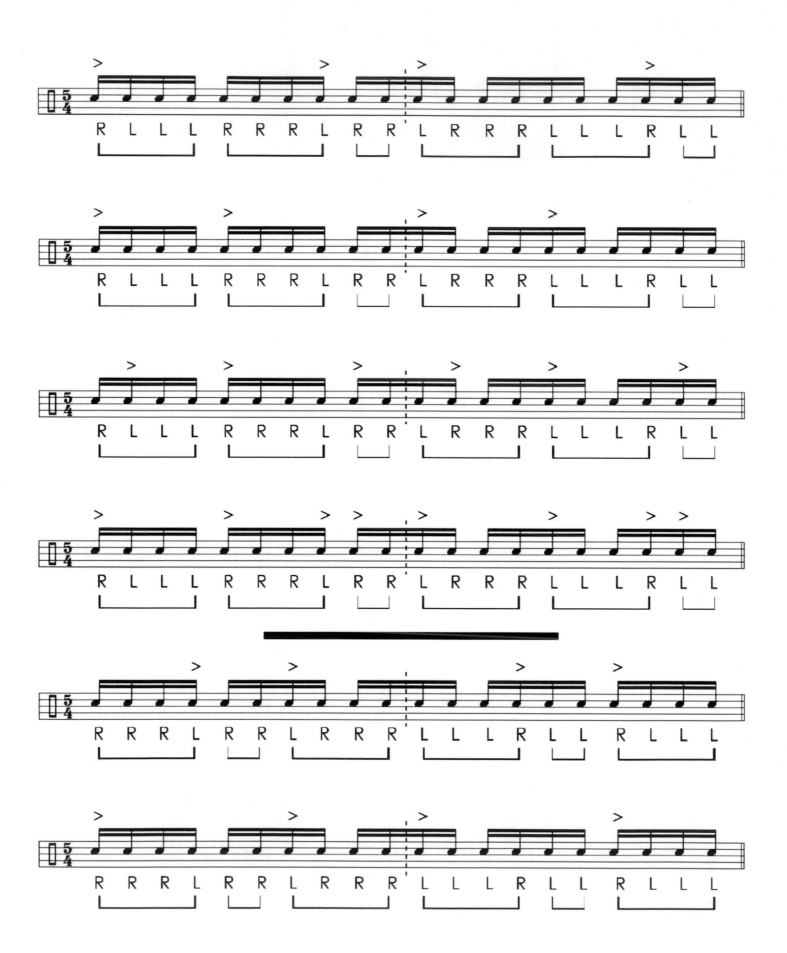

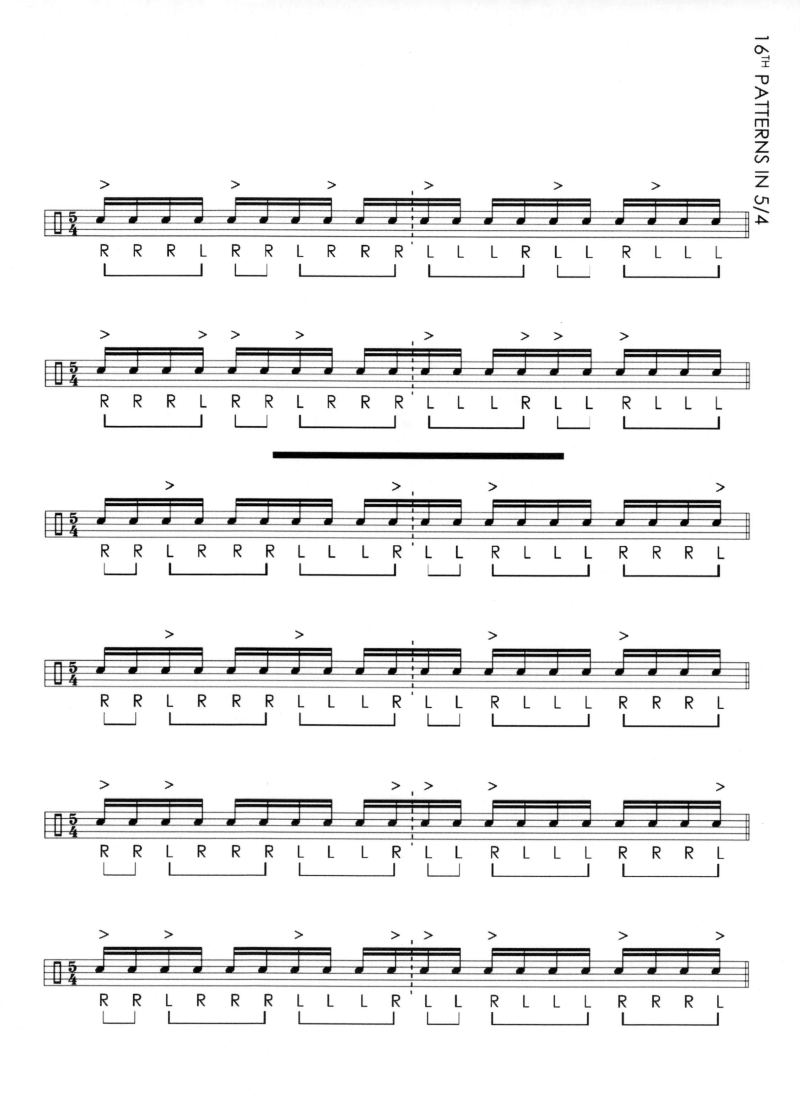

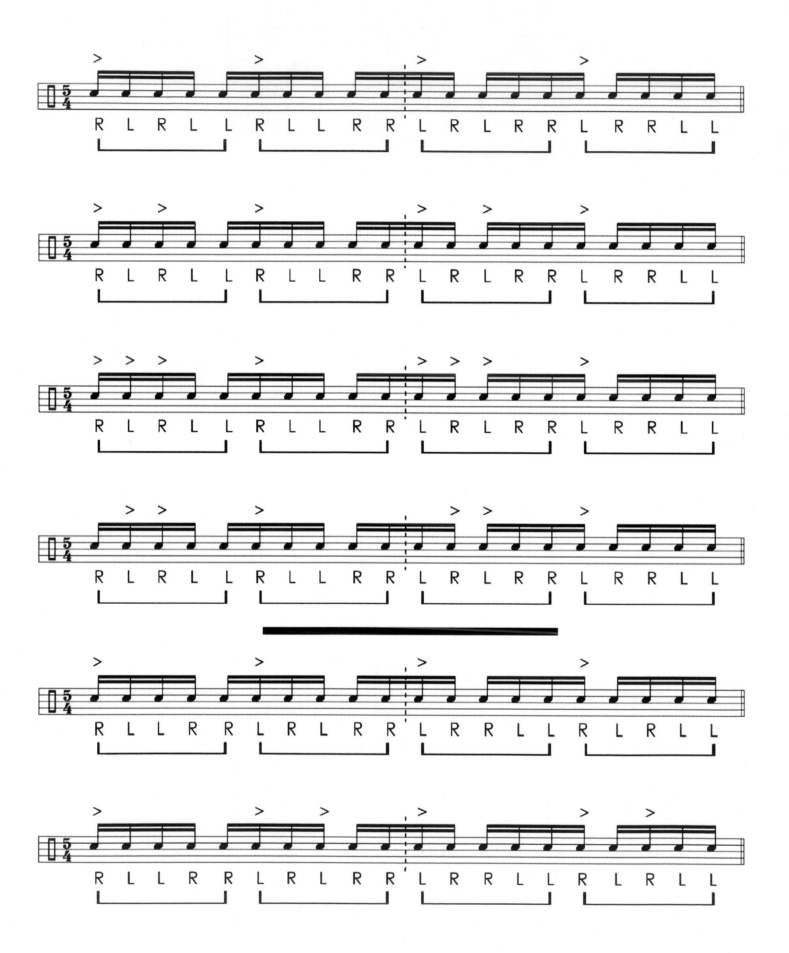

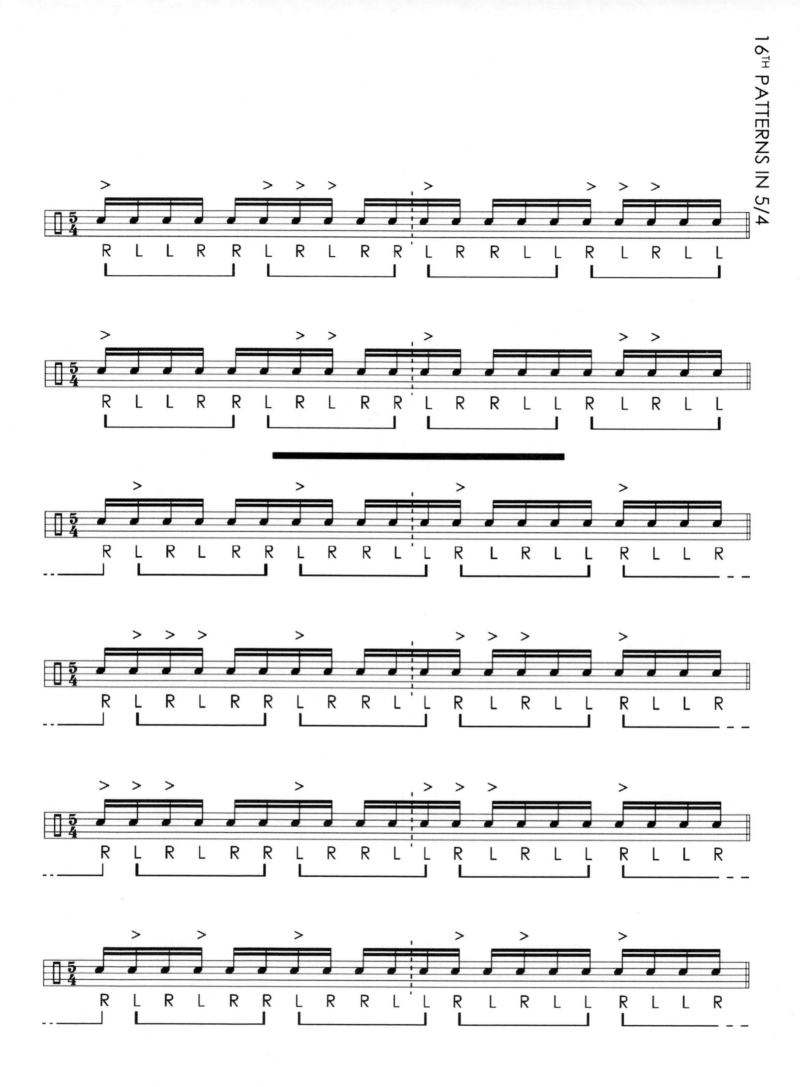

16th PATTERNS IN 7/4

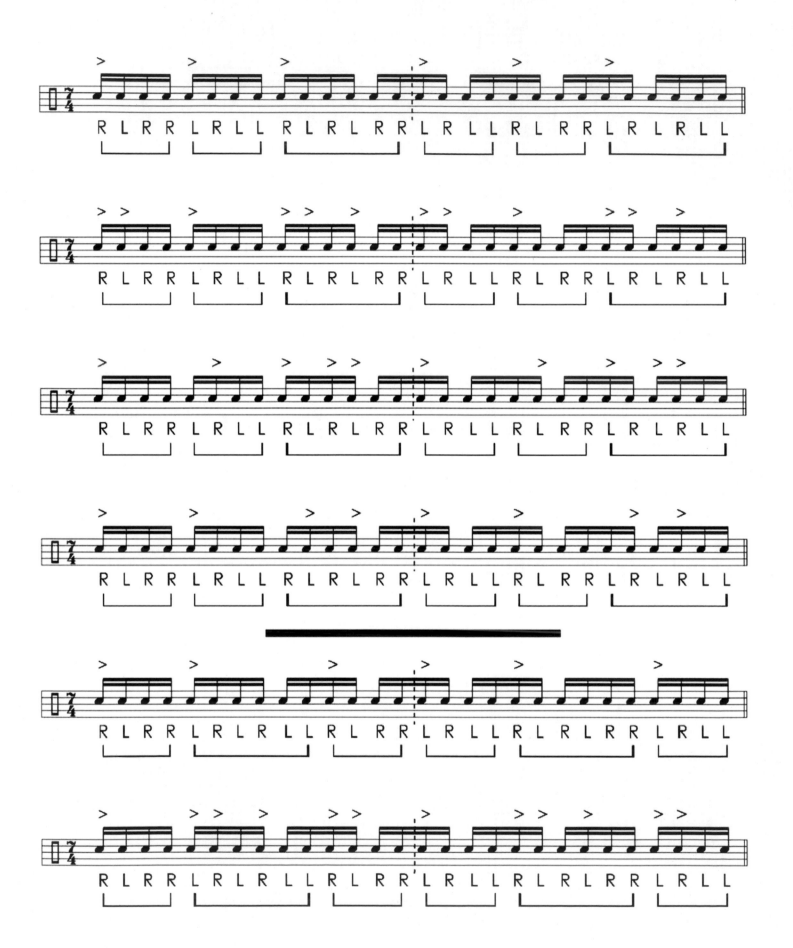

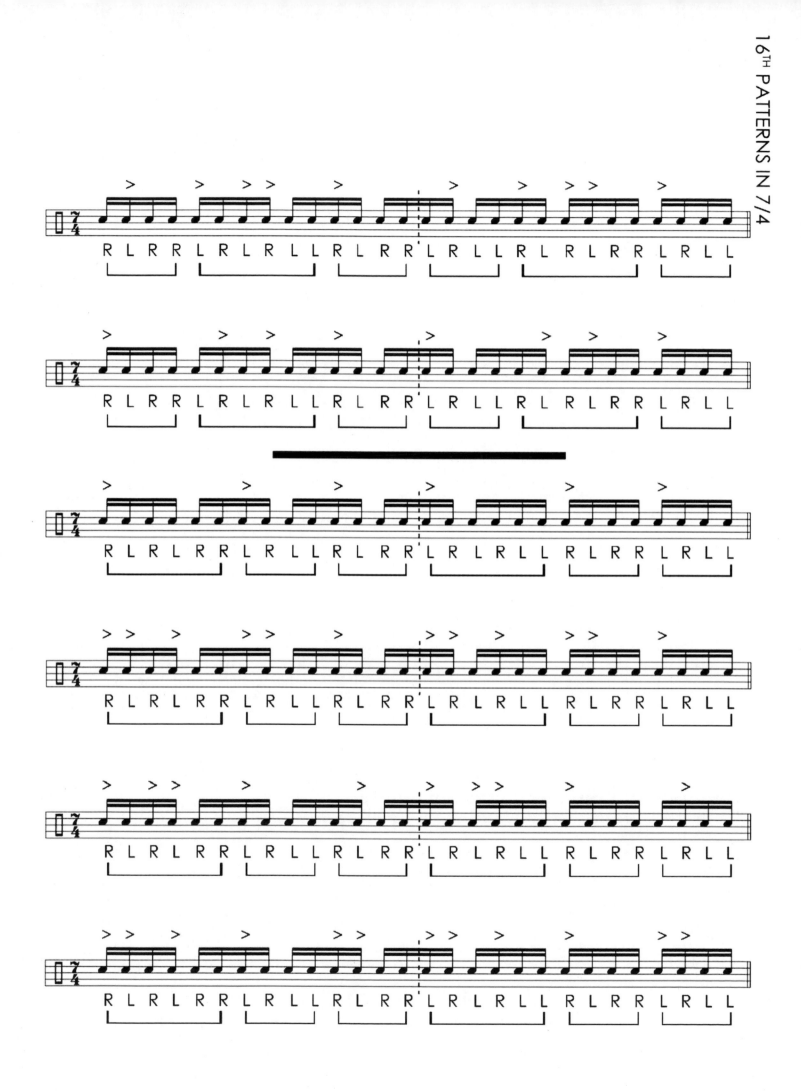

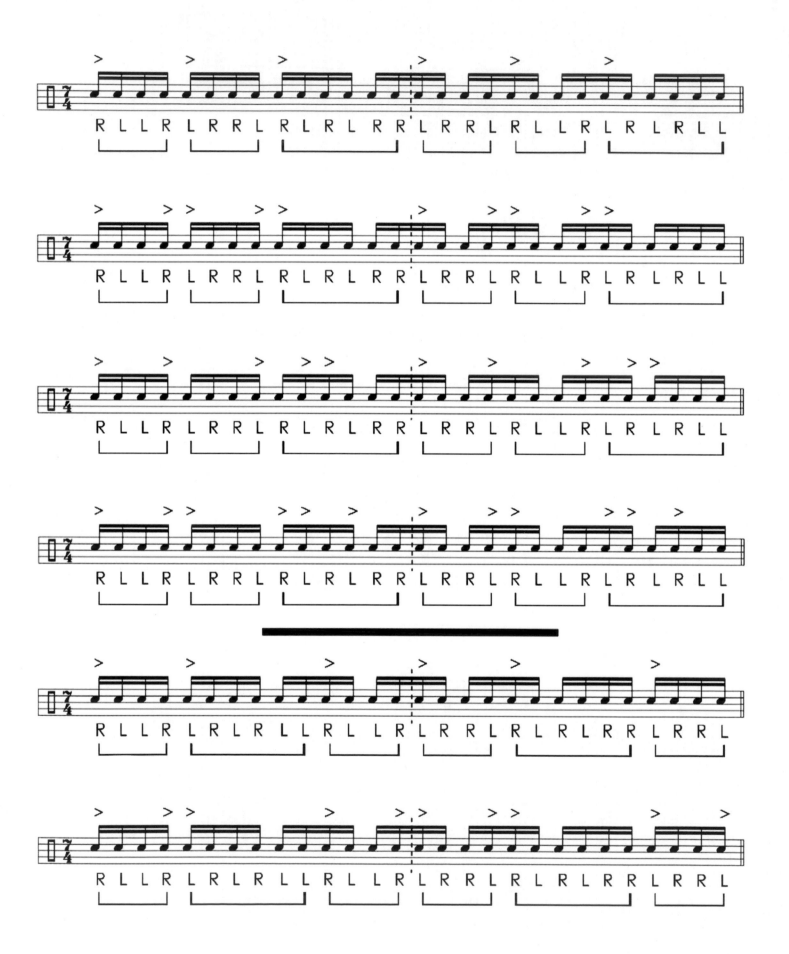

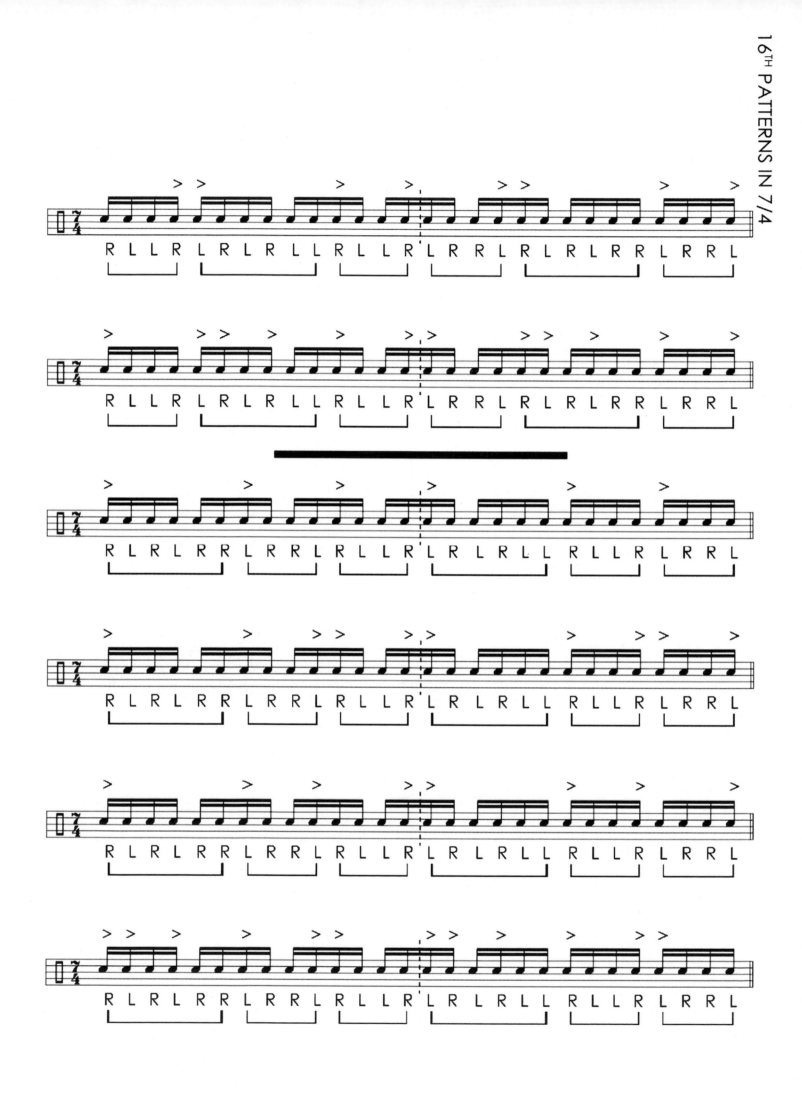

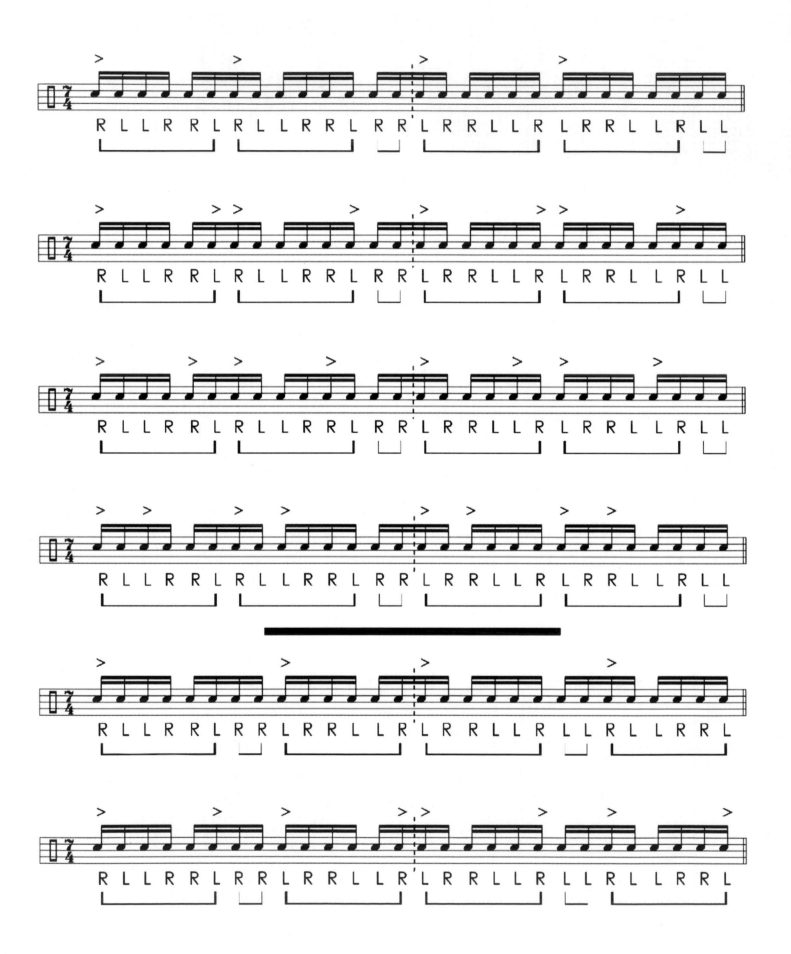

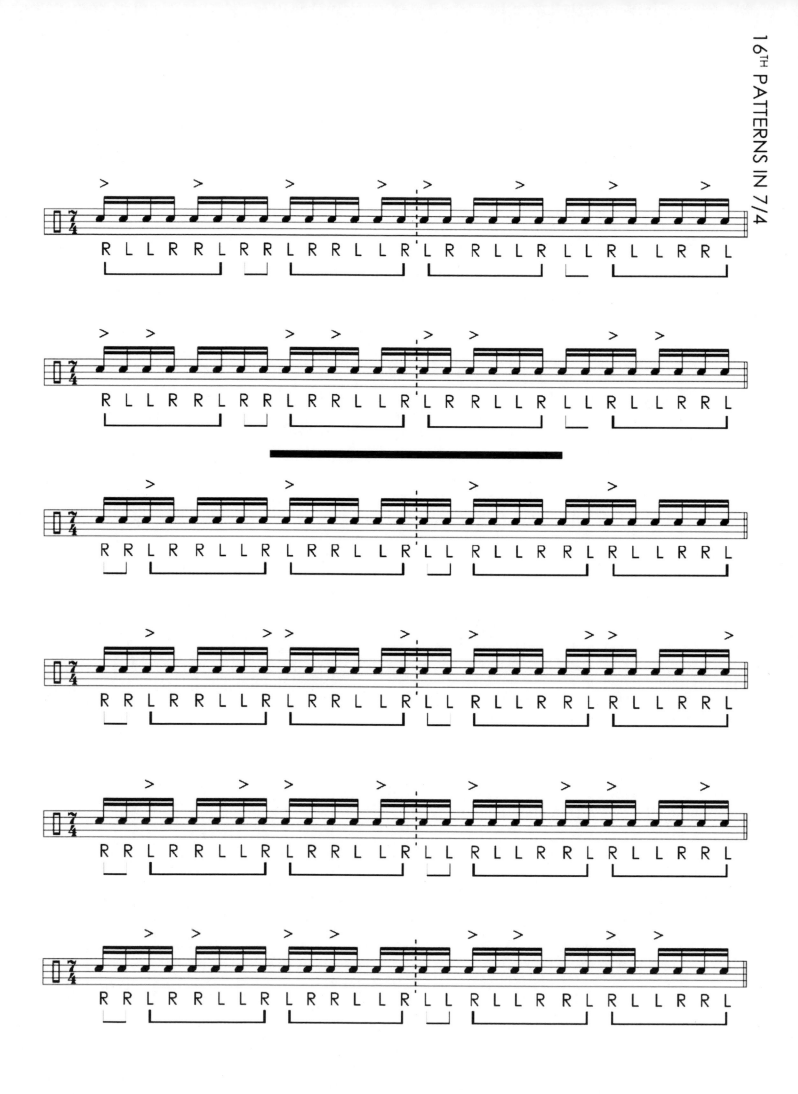

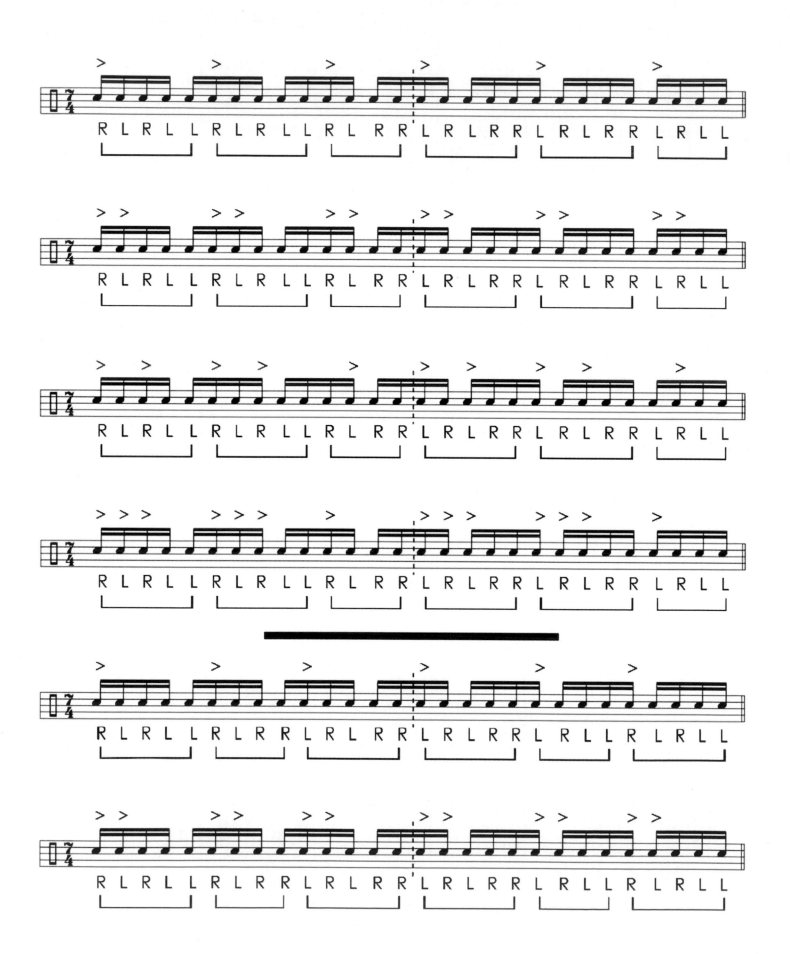

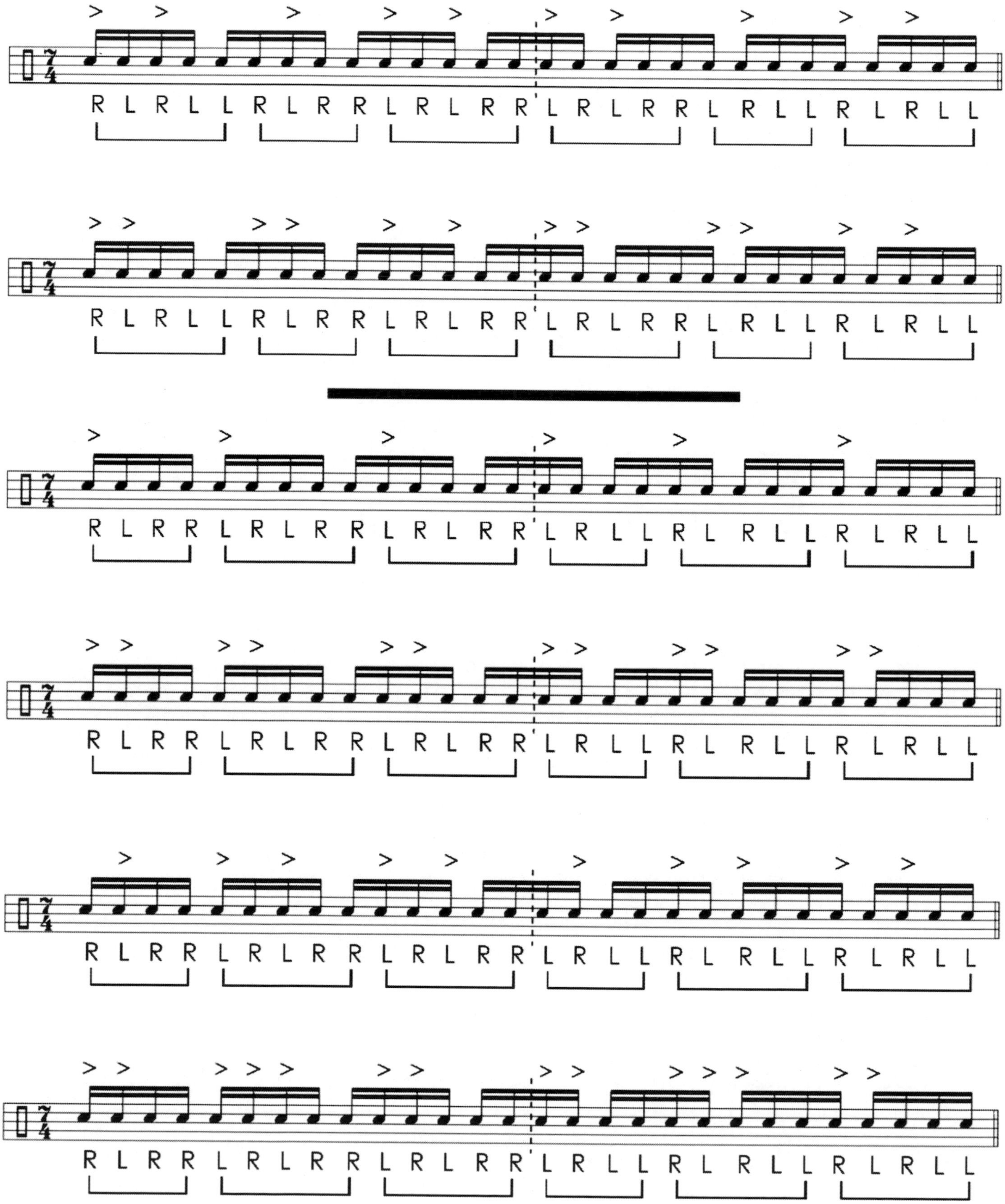

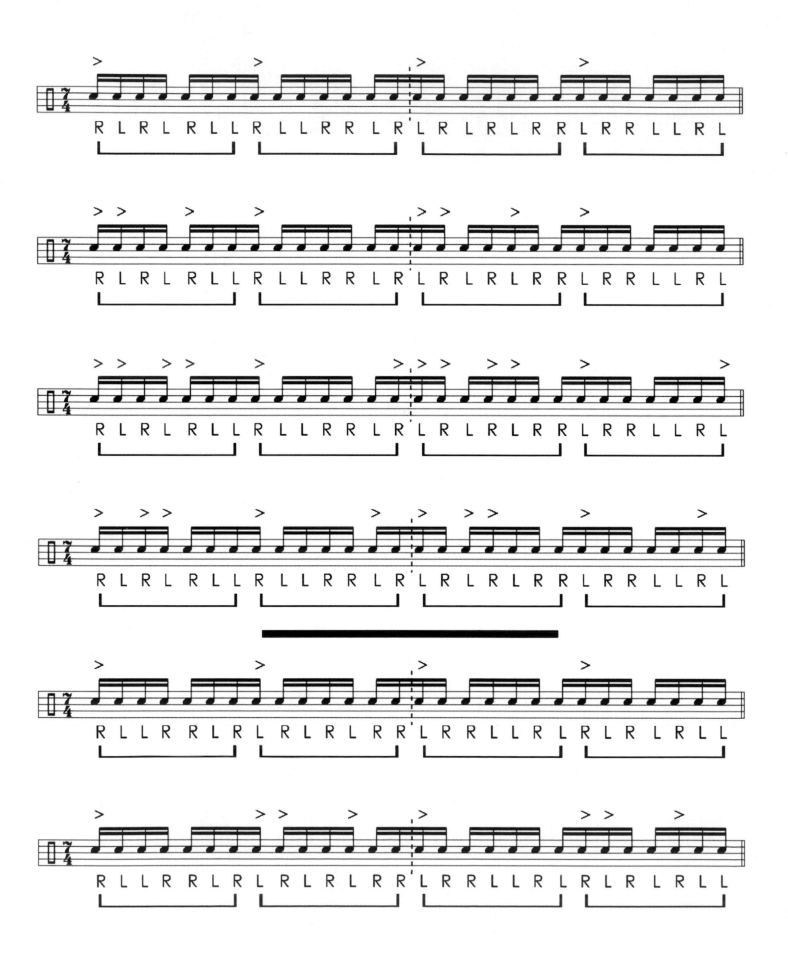

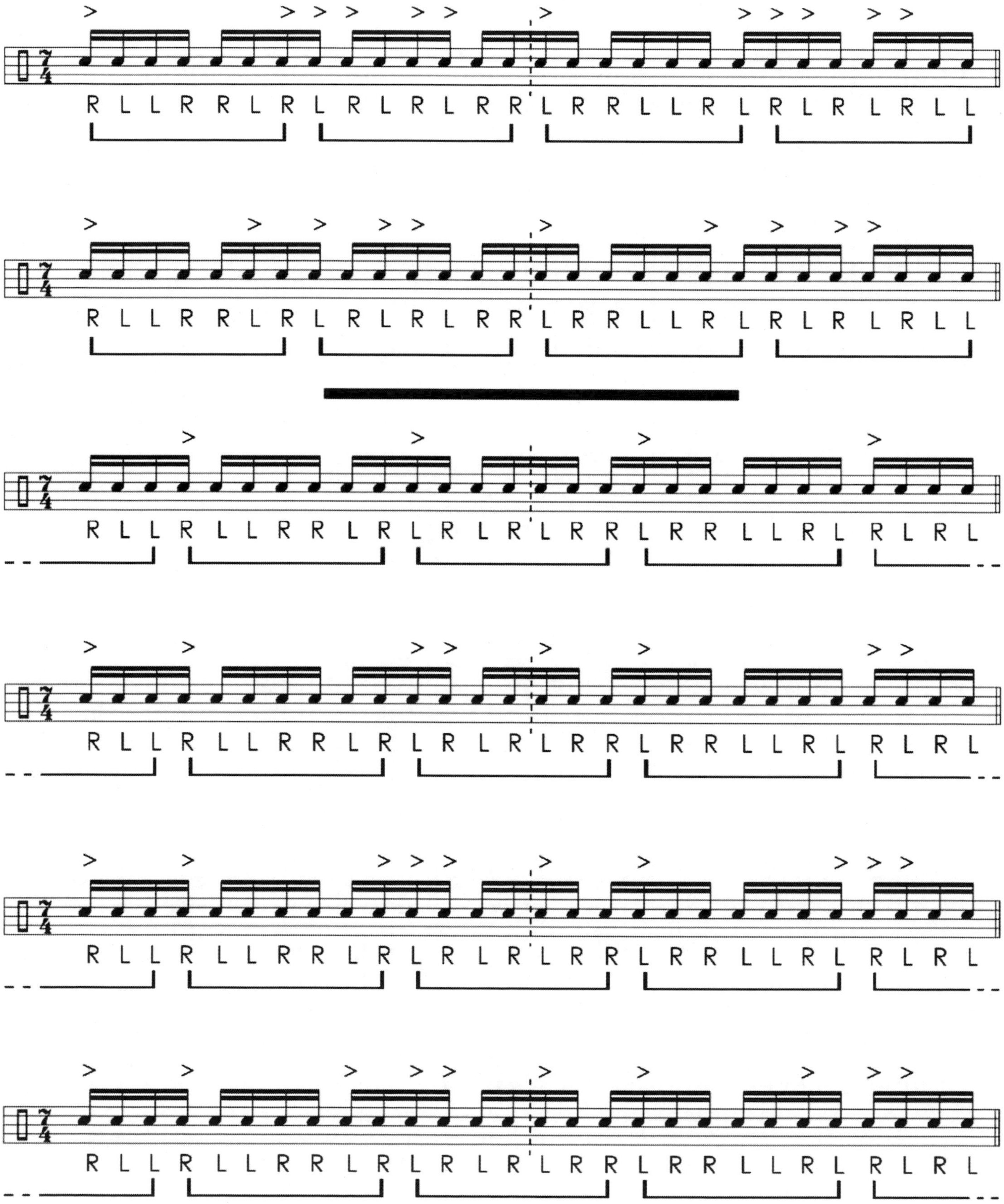
R L L R R L R L R L R L R R L R R L L R L R L R L R L L
R L L R R L R L R L R L R R L R R L L R L R L R L R L L
R L L R L L R R L R L R L R L R R L R R L L R L R L R L
R L L R L L R R L R L R L R L R R L R R L L R L R L R L
R L L R L L R R L R L R L R L R R L R R L L R L R L R L
R L L R L L R R L R L R L R L R R L R R L L R L R L R L

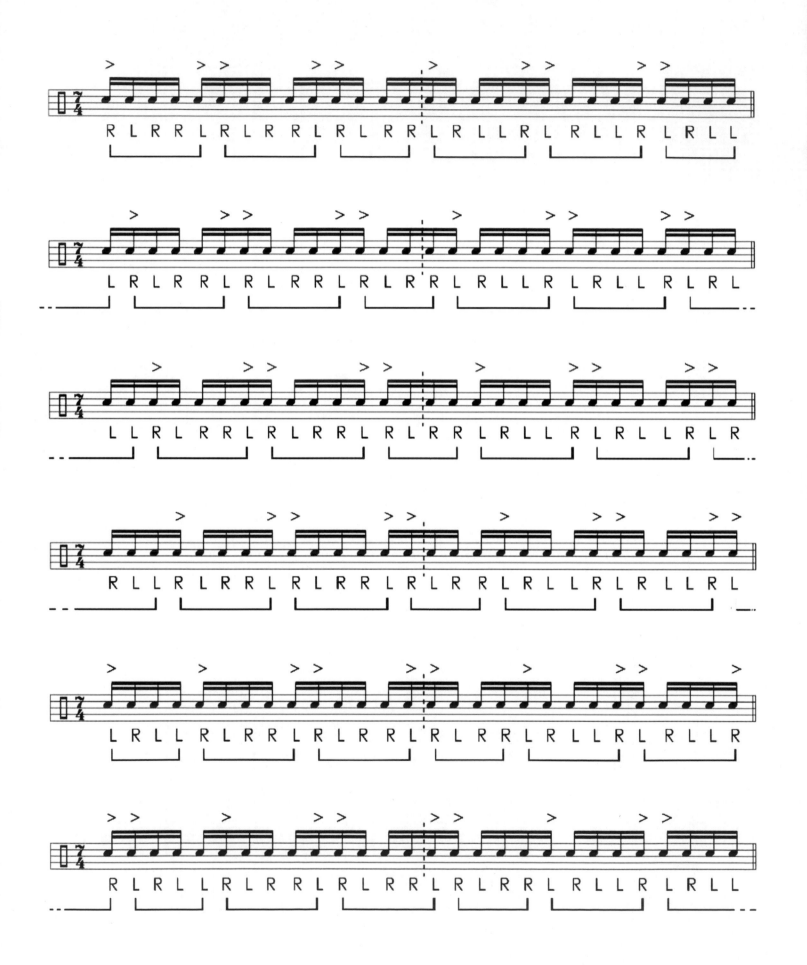

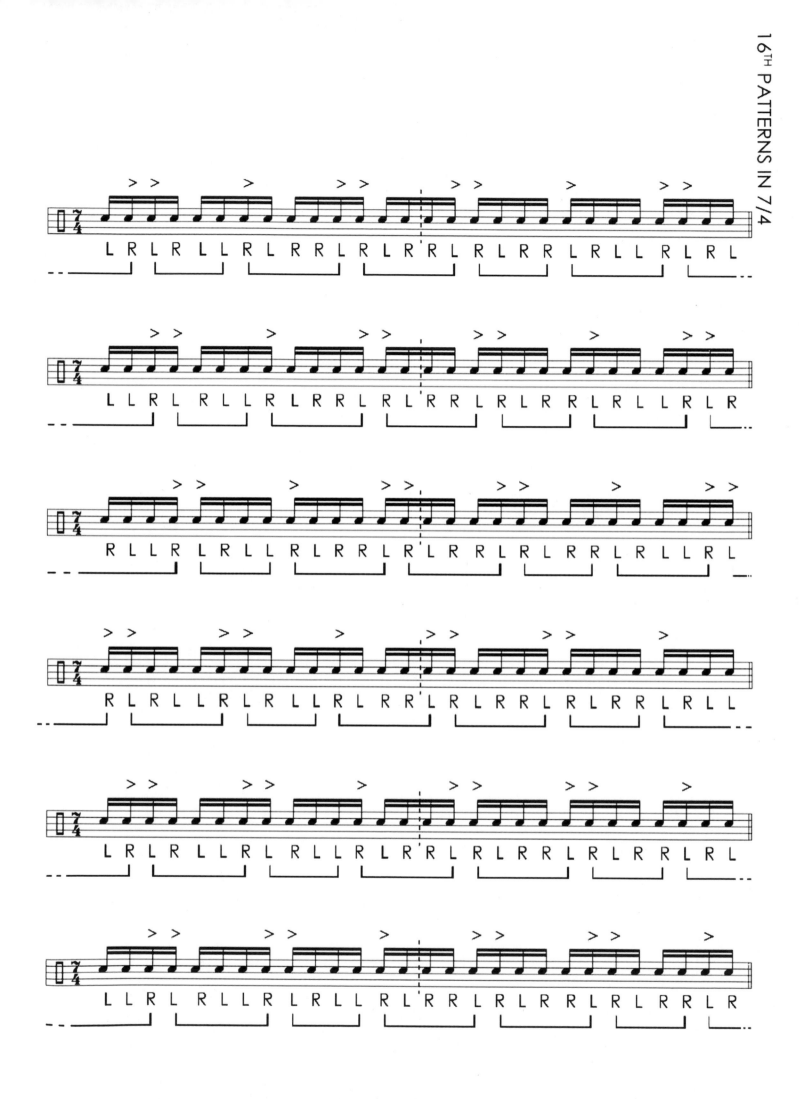